TRANSFORMING
SCHOOL
CULTURE

How to Overcome
Staff Division

Anthony MUHAMMAD

foreword by *Richard DuFour*

Solution Tree | Press

a division of

Solution Tree

555 North Morton Street
Bloomington, IN 47404
800.733.6786 (toll free) / 812.336.7700
FAX: 812.336.7790

email: info@solution-tree.com
solution-tree.com

Printed in the United States of America

Library of Congress Control Number: 2008943515

14 13 12 11   8   9   10

FSC
Mixed Sources
Product group from well-managed
forests and other controlled sources
Cert no. SW-COC-002283
www.fsc.org
© 1996 Forest Stewardship Council

Library of Congress Cataloging-in-Publication Data

Muhammad, Anthony.
  Transforming school culture : how to overcome staff division / Anthony
Muhammad.
    p. cm.
  Includes bibliographical references.
  ISBN 978-1-935249-05-4 (lib. bdg.) -- ISBN 978-1-934009-45-1 -- ISBN
978-1-934009-99-4 (ebook)
  1. Educational leadership. 2. School environment. 3. Educational
change 4. Educational accountability. 5. School improvement programs.
I. Title.
  LB2805.M75 2009
  371.2 '01--dc22
                              2008054537

Solution Tree
Jeffrey C. Jones, CEO and President

Solution Tree Press
President: Douglas M. Rife
Publisher: Robert D. Clouse
Director of Production: Gretchen Knapp
Managing Production Editor: Caroline Wise
Senior Production Editor: Suzanne Kraszewski
Text Designer: Raven Bongiani
Cover Designer: Orlando Angel

Dedication

This book is dedicated to every child who has been doubted. To all of the children in housing projects, barrios, cities, and countrysides who feel that life is hopeless, it is not hopeless! If a young man from the north end of Flint, Michigan, can be an educated scholar, the sky is the limit for you. Keep your head held high, and show the world your talent. As long as I have a breath in my body, I will fight for you, but you have to fight for yourself, too.

—Anthony Muhammad

Acknowledgments

The acknowledgments for this book could easily be as long as the text. I have been so abundantly blessed, and there are so many people who have helped me grow in my short time here on this earth. First and foremost, I must give praise and all of the credit for anything worthwhile to Almighty God, the creator of all things. He has guided every step I have ever taken and every thought that I have ever produced, and to Him all praise is due.

I must acknowledge and thank the love and influence of my grandmother, Emma Robinson-Harper (Madear), the matriarch of our family, the rock that we love and on whom we rely. Special thanks to Anna Harper-Nelson, my mother, nurturer, and friend. Donald Crawford, my father and twin, thanks for your spirit and DNA; we are much more alike than we would ever admit. Thanks to Andrew Nelson, Sr.; I appreciate you raising a son that you did not conceive when others would have run the other way. A special, special thanks goes to my beautiful wife Dronda. I appreciate you showing me the other side of life and for all of your patience, love, and support. Carmen, thanks for giving me the four greatest gifts that a man could ever receive. Rashad, Larry, Jamilah, Shaheed, Ayanna, and Logan, the sun rises and sets on you. There is nothing that I would not do for you. Do not be afraid to take on the world and become what God created you to be. Angie, Lee, Donald, Brandon, and Derek (R.I.P.), thanks for supporting your big brother. Cookie, Wendy, Billie, Peter, Birdie, Ricky, and Lori, thanks for supporting your nephew. Thanks to the entire Harper, Crawford, and Nelson families for your support and love. Thanks to the Gilliam/ Hale family for accepting me into your family and giving me love and support. Finally, I would like to give special acknowledgement to my hometown of Flint, Michigan, the greatest place in the world for a young man to grow up. Wherever life takes me, I will be a Flintstone for life!

From a professional standpoint, I would like to thank the following powerful influences. Again, thank you, Mom, for being a great teacher and a great educational role model. I would like to express special appreciation to Dr. Richard DuFour for being a role model, mentor, friend, and one of the best educators this nation has ever produced. Becky DuFour and Robert Eaker, thank you for your guidance and willingness to share your wisdom with me. I would like to express appreciation to Jeff Jones, Donald "Stubby" McLean, and the entire Solution Tree staff. Dr. Freya Rivers, the first master teacher I ever observed, thank you for pushing and encouraging me, even when we did not agree. I would like to give a special acknowledgement to the Southfield, Michigan, Public Schools for your support and confidence, especially the very special staff, students, and parents at Levey Middle School, the greatest middle school on the planet. Finally, I would like to acknowledge all of the educators at Michigan State University for their wisdom and guidance.

Table of Contents

About the Author

Anthony Muhammad, Ph.D., is a much sought-after educational consultant. Dr. Muhammad, a practitioner for nearly 20 years, served as a middle school teacher, assistant principal, middle school principal, and high school principal. Dr. Muhammad's tenure as a practitioner has earned him several awards as both a teacher and a principal. His most notable accomplishment came as principal at Levey Middle School in Southfield, Michigan, a National School of Excellence, where student proficiency on state assessments more than doubled in 5 years. Dr. Muhammad and the staff at Levey used the Professional Learning Communities at Work (PLC) model of school improvement, and they have been recognized in several videos and articles as a model high-performing PLC. As a researcher, Dr. Muhammad has published articles in several publications in both the United States and Canada. He is a contributing author in *The Collaborative Administrator: Working Together as a Professional Learning Community* (2008).

Foreword

By Richard DuFour, Educational Author and Consultant

Add the name of Dr. Anthony Muhammad to the growing list of educational researchers who have concluded that schools will not meet the unprecedented challenge of helping *all* students learn at high levels unless educators establish very different school cultures. Structural changes—changes in policy, programs, and procedures—will only take a school so far. Substantive and sustainable school improvement will require educators to consider, address, and ultimately transform school culture—the assumptions, beliefs, expectations, and habits that constitute the norm for their schools.

Dr. Muhammad does more, however, than urge educators to address culture; he provides them with a framework and strategies for doing so. He points out, rightly, that in an organization as complex as a school, there is rarely a single "norm" that is embraced universally by the members of the staff. There are, instead, *competing* assumptions, beliefs, expectations, and diversity of opinion regarding such basic questions as what is the fundamental purpose of this school, what are my responsibilities as an educator, and what is the school we should strive to create?

Dr. Muhammad draws upon his study of 34 schools from around the country—11 elementary, 14 middle, and 9 high schools—to describe this competition as an underlying tension among four different groups of educators in a school. Much of the book is devoted to introducing readers to those groups. The Fundamentalists are preservers of the status quo. They were successful as students in the traditional school culture, and they resent any attempts to change it. The Believers are those who are committed to the learning of each student and who operate under the assumption that their efforts can make an enormous difference in that learning. The Tweeners are members of a staff who are typically new to a school and are attempting to learn its prevailing culture. The Survivors are those who have been so overwhelmed by the stress and demands of the profession that their primary goal becomes making it through the day, the week, and the year.

Dr. Muhammad describes the prevailing beliefs and assumptions of each of these groups. No one who has ever worked in a school will be able to read his descriptions without conjuring up images of specific colleagues who fall into each category. More importantly, he describes the dynamics within and among the groups and argues that it is the outcome of this dynamic that will ultimately determine the culture of a school.

There is much to admire in this book. For example, I appreciated the fact that Dr. Muhammad does not denigrate the members of any group. He describes educators as "intelligent and concerned" and acknowledges that each group is acting in accordance with what it perceives as its best interest. He emphasizes that a sense of moral purpose and the desire to help all students learn does not ensure an individual teacher is effective. He recognizes that an individual's commitment to preserving the status quo does not make that person an ineffective classroom teacher. He found very effective classroom teachers among the Fundamentalists and very ineffective teachers among Believers, despite their good intentions. He does not depict the tension between the factions in a school as a battle of good versus evil, but rather as a struggle between real people who are merely acting in accordance with their view of the world. He is, however, emphatic in his conclusion that without changing the prevailing assumptions in most schools, educators cannot fulfill their stated purpose of helping all students learn. Thus, he sets out to help readers understand those different worldviews and offers suggestions regarding how they might be shaped.

This willingness to do more than stress the importance of culture, but to present practical ideas and recommendations for influencing the existing assumptions, beliefs, expectations, and habits in a school is another of the book's strengths. Dr. Muhammad uses the research of Karl Weick to examine the different reasons people resist change. He then offers specific strategies for addressing each of those reasons. He acknowledges there is no magic bullet that causes instant transformation, but instead advises school principals and teacher leaders regarding how they can slowly, incrementally influence assumptions and expectations until they create new norms for their schools.

Finally, the book is particularly powerful because the author has not merely studied the challenge of changing a school's culture; he has actually done it in an extraordinarily successful way. Dr. Muhammad, a former Principal of the Year for the state of Michigan, led a staff in transforming a high-poverty, high-minority school with a toxic culture of low expectations and a tradition of miserable student achievement into a nationally recognized school that serves as a model for successfully closing the achievement gap. When Dr. Muhammad states that a "dysfunctional or 'toxic' school culture is not insurmountable," he does so with the absolute conviction of someone who has been spectacularly successful in taking on that challenge.

Be forewarned that this book is provocative. Dr. Muhammad offers bold statements, and it is very likely that you will not concur with all of his observations and conclusions. You will, however, be required to think and to examine your own beliefs.

For too long educators have given lip service to the idea of creating schools where all kids learn at high levels. For too long we have devoted time to developing pious mission statements rather than aligning our practices with that mission. For too long we have tinkered with the structures of our schools and focused on projects or goals that have no impact on student learning. For too long we have ignored the elephant in the room and avoided the crucial conversations regarding the assumptions, expectations, and beliefs that underlie our practices. Dr. Muhammad issues a passionate call for all educators to confront the fierce urgency of now and to take meaningful steps that breathe new life into schools and the students they serve. I urge you to read this book and heed his words.

CHAPTER 1

From Status Quo to True Reform

For more than a century, educators, scholars, politicians, and citizens have debated the purpose of our public school system and how best to reform it. Ironically, our public school system has undergone sweeping changes in the 20th century and beyond, yet it has remained largely the same, and there is still a lack of clear consensus about what is needed to ensure that all of our schools perform at high levels and all of our students achieve success.

Education has traditionally been viewed as the best route for social mobility, but for some young people, this route is not accessible. In fact, as an abundance of data on the costs of this failure of our education system show, the system is absolutely broken. This is especially true for children from certain demographic groups who have been traditionally underserved by our school system.

Persistent gaps between white and African American citizens in critical areas like income, health, and education have been important issues at the center of debates about equity for a long time. A 2006 U.S. Census Bureau report (Infoplease, 2006) found that 43% of African American youth live in homes that have incomes at or below the national poverty line. Sixty-five percent of African American children live in homes headed by single parents. Teen pregnancy rates among African American girls are twice the rate of white girls. Of the nearly two million incarcerated Americans, African American males account for nearly 900,000 of the inmates, and 84% of those inmates are functionally illiterate. Rates of HIV/AIDS infections among African Americans are twice that of white Americans.

The Latino population in America has grown rapidly, and Latinos now represent the largest ethnic minority group in the United States. America's Latino population is now facing the issues that have plagued African Americans, including a gap in student performance with white students on standardized academic assessments. The same U.S. Census Bureau report (Infoplease, 2006) indicated that the median Latino household income was $34,000 annually, which was $6,000 below the national average and $8,000 below the median income for white families. Latino poverty rates were 10% above the national average and 14% higher than the average for white families. Latinos also experienced significantly lower employment levels as well as an increased risk of health issues such as diabetes, hypertension, and heart disease.

However, race is just one risk factor. Students from poor families, regardless of their racial group, are experiencing the significant costs of a poor education. The U.S. Census Bureau (Infoplease, 2006) also reported that economically disadvantaged white households (those with incomes below the national poverty line) had significant gaps in income, employment, and health compared to national averages, though not as pronounced as African Americans and Latinos. And there is evidence that poverty can put children more at risk for outcomes even more serious than future low income and unemployment. A 2005 study conducted by Christopher Hudson with more than 34,000 patients with mental illness proved that children who grow up in impoverished homes are significantly more likely to develop mental illness than children who grow up in homes with incomes above the national poverty line. Hudson wrote, "The poorer one's socioeconomic conditions are, the higher one's risk is for mental disability and psychiatric hospitalization" (Hudson, 2005, p. 14).

Henry Levin (2006) has identified links between high school graduation and quality of life. While analyzing the effects of failing to complete high school, he found that minority students and students of poverty have much lower graduation rates than the national average. In fact, African American and Latino students graduate from high school at a rate slightly above 50% (compared to the national graduation rate of 70%), while economically disadvantaged students graduate at a rate of 63%. He found that adults without a high school diploma are twice as likely to be unemployed as high school graduates. The life expectancy of a high school dropout as compared to a graduate is 9.2 years lower, and the average 65-year-old high school graduate is in better health than the average 45-year-old high school dropout. Finally, Levin found that 70% of those sitting in our nation's prisons are high school dropouts. In the words of the crew aboard the Apollo 13 spacecraft, "Houston, we have a problem!" The youth who need education most to provide a catalyst for creating positive change in their lives are those who persistently achieve at the lowest levels in our schools.

Challenges of the 21st Century

As Thomas Friedman acknowledges in his book *The World is Flat* (2005), the landscape of the new century has changed. Foreign competition, especially in the area of technology and science, has increased substantially. As corporations struggle to find educated and skilled workers, they are looking to the shores of foreign nations more and more. Friedman points to the increase in technology worldwide as a catalyst for a world without borders. The Internet, satellites, and global technology have made it possible for workers to utilize their talents from a foreign shore without ever setting foot in the United States.

What does this mean for the American economy? Corporations, by nature, seek to be profitable. They want to maximize productivity and minimize expenses. The days of industrial plants filled with high-paying, low-skill jobs are over. The safety net for those who occupy the lowest space on the educational and societal bell curve is gone. Companies are seeking employees who have academic skills, common sense, and social skills, and if they have to recruit overseas to accomplish this, they are willing to do so. Nations like India and China are providing workers who have the kind of skills that companies want, and they are increasing their recruitment efforts globally in order to fill this need.

This is especially bad news for our nation's poor and disenfranchised. With more skilled workers making their entrance into the global workforce, education is more critical than ever. As the data show, opportunities are already limited for poor and minority citizens in the United States, and globalization signifies more of the same.

We should never consider education a luxury; it is a necessity, especially for children in poor and minority communities, so that they can some day enjoy a high quality of life. It may be their only chance at a better life. So why are the schools that serve these students, on average, in the worst condition, and why do they have the lowest levels of funding and academic achievement? School funding for the typical urban public school is on average 30% less than suburban schools that serve primarily white middle-class students. The gap in achievement on standardized test results in math and reading between urban and suburban students averages around 22% (Allen, 2007). In fact, a group of students from the Chicago Public Schools boycotted the first day of school in protest of the huge funding disparity between the per-pupil funding in Chicago ($10,400) and the nearby suburban district of New Trier Township ($17,000) (Sadovi, 2008).

So what does all this mean for American schools? It means that they have to respond like never before. Michael Fullan writes in *Moral Imperative of School Leadership* (2003), "The best case for public education has always been that it is a common good. Everyone ultimately has a stake in the caliber of schools, and education is everyone's business" (p. 14). The United States built its reputation and status worldwide on the backs of its citizens' ingenuity and work ethic. With other nations now seeking to distinguish themselves among the world's elite, how will our schools respond? Do we simply believe that we are entitled to world admiration, or will our schools and our society rise to the occasion and produce better results—more skilled and focused students?

If the United States is to maintain its position in the world, the quality of education and academic skills of its students must improve. In addition, more students—not just white, middle-class, and affluent students—have to develop educationally so that America can continue to compete and be a viable force in our new global economy. Racism and class bias cannot be obstacles that interfere with education, but unfortunately they are. "Education for all" is not just a liberal rant; it is a matter of survival for everyone, but especially those groups that have been pushed into the margins of society.

No Child Left Behind

The reauthorization in 2001 of the Elementary and Secondary Education Act (ESEA), also known as No Child Left Behind (NCLB), symbolized a huge shift in the focus of American schools. This bill, which requires that all students in America's public schools perform at a proficient level on each state's standardized assessment in reading and mathematics by 2014 or face sanctions, sent a shockwave through the U.S. public school system.

The introduction of this legislation meant that for the first time in U.S. history, schools would be judged based upon *student outcomes,* not *educator intentions.* There has been a lot of debate about the effects of NCLB and where we go from here. Many wonder if a governmental mandate is enough to change long-standing gaps in student achievement and change the nature of teaching and learning in the classroom. This is a very good question. In fact, since the implementation of NCLB, we have seen no significant progress in closing achievement gaps in student performance and have made no real steps in realizing the fair and equitable system the legislation aims to accomplish.

According to the data from the 2007 National Assessment of Educational Progress (NAEP), students from inner-city schools are making modest gains in the areas of math and reading, especially in the early grades, compared to NAEP achievement levels over the past 7 years, but absolutely no progress in secondary grades in the same period. These incremental gains in the early grades are admirable, but they are not growing at the same rate as gains made in economically affluent suburban schools with majority white and Asian populations, so even small signs of progress have done little to close performance gaps between inner-city and suburban students (Zuckerbrod, 2007). And the fear of accountability and embarrassment has placed serious scrutiny on the data itself. Since NCLB, districts have become increasingly savvy at hiding their struggling students or finding ways to omit them altogether. A 2006 study found that over two million student scores, almost exclusively minority and socioeconomically disadvantaged students, were "mysteriously omitted" from state test reporting data to the federal government (Dizon, Feller, & Bass, 2006).

To add insult to injury, an Associated Press poll found that the majority of teachers (58%) felt that being expected to ensure that all of their children read and perform mathematics at grade level was unrealistic and impossible to accomplish (Feller, 2006). Organizational protection for marginally performing teachers has also made implementing the goals of NCLB difficult. A study of five large school systems conducted by the New York Teacher Project Fund found that union staffing rules often allow veteran teachers to transfer to new assignments without giving administrators a say in the matter. Because it is difficult to fire poorly performing teachers, principals often move such employees from school to school. As a result, many urban schools are forced to staff their schools with teachers who are not wanted elsewhere. Michelle Rhee, the president of the study's sponsoring organization, stated that "without changing these labor rules, urban schools will never be in a position to sustain meaningful school reform" (Helfand, 2005, p. 1). These facts should make us question our seriousness as a profession and as a nation about creating schools that guarantee learning for all students.

The goals of NCLB are admirable and morally correct, but we must acknowledge that breaking a system of normally distributed achievement is not going to end with the stroke of a legislative pen. In *Tinkering Towards Utopia* (1995), a watershed book on the history of educational reform in the United States, Larry Cuban and David Tyack clearly establish that educational reform is very difficult to establish, and very little has changed in the American education system of the past century. Cuban and Tyack point to the complex nature of our society along with the ever-changing definition of the purpose of public schools as causing a stalemate that is very difficult to overcome. These issues are woven into the fabric of American public education. A solid, realistic plan of action that aggressively addresses these issues is necessary for true reform.

The Dawn of a New Day: High Anxiety

I first heard of NCLB on an ordinary Friday morning in March of 2002 while serving as a middle school principal in an urban school district with more than 98% minority enrollment. I was on my way to the district administrative office for our biweekly administrator's meeting, called the "pay-day meeting." It was 8:05 a.m., and I was 5 minutes late, as usual. I was expecting an agenda filled with mundane administrative logistics and announcements. I anticipated the superintendent leading the meeting, as he usually did, with concerns about our budget or some security issue from a sporting event. There was no way I could have anticipated the topic of this meeting.

As I entered the room, the superintendent introduced an official from the Michigan Department of Education who came to share some information from the federal government. As she explained the goals and components of a new law, NCLB, there was an eerie silence in the room coupled with a universal feeling of shock and anxiety.

The goals of this law were not incongruent with what we, as administrators, wanted for each one of our students, but we never suspected that we would actually be held legally accountable for producing schools that made these wishes a reality. The state official went on to explain that schools that did not meet these requirements would be labeled as "failing" and would face a series of sanctions.

Everyone at the meeting was shocked. Our effectiveness or proficiency would be judged primarily by student outcomes on standardized tests and our ability to move our entire school organization to accept this new reality. We had been introduced to the new reality of American education. After examining our current reality, it seemed we had to be miracle workers to bring this new reality to fruition.

Why was there so much shock and anxiety among this group of administrators? Primarily, we were anxious because we were painfully aware of the culture and history of our schools. We were aware of what we assumed government officials were not. We were aware of all the issues surrounding teacher quality, staff expectations, student apathy, and inadequate parental support, among other things that we had worked so hard to keep away from the public eye. We had been trained to create an illusion of prosperity that we never expected to actually achieve. We knew that there were many classrooms where the curriculum was not followed. We knew that gaps in student performance were expected in a traditional urban public school system. We were being asked to do something that no one had ever been asked to do: create a functional system in which every child could learn and would learn, despite the many obstacles and the myriad of tasks necessary just to be functional. It was absolutely overwhelming, and we did not know where to start. In fact, we banked on the assumption that if we ignored this new law long enough, it would eventually just go away.

Clearly it has not gone away, and years later the same anxiety exists. We are just as confused today as we were on that memorable Friday morning in 2002. Student performance has improved very little, and the dysfunction in our education system that faced us in 2002 is still prevalent. In fact, U.S. Secretary of Education Margaret Spellings told a group of businesspeople in Detroit that "we can't adequately solve this problem [the achievement gap] until we diagnose what's wrong" (Higgins & Pratt-Dawsey, 2008, p. 1). Many years and several billion dollars later, our best educational minds are still diagnosing the problem. Improving public schools is very complex indeed.

As Margaret Spellings pointed out, understanding and diagnosing the problem will help us start the much-needed process of reconstructing our schools so that the organization meets the varied needs of all students. This book contends that this very difficult journey begins with the adults, the professionals, taking an honest look at how this gap in student performance began and how it is perpetuated despite the honest efforts of very intelligent and concerned people. Universal achievement remains a pipe dream until we take an honest look at our beliefs, practices, behaviors, and the norms of our organization. These elements make up a very sensitive system known as a school's culture. This is where many school officials and reformers fear to tread, but it is this place that holds the biggest keys to unlocking the potential of our public schools.

School Culture Research

According to Kent D. Peterson, a professor in the Department of Educational Leadership and Policy Analysis at the University of Wisconsin-Madison, "School culture is the set of norms, values and beliefs, rituals and ceremonies, symbols and stories that make up the 'persona' of the school" (Cromwell, 2002, p. 4). School culture is a rather recent field of study. For years, we did not consider how the varied and diverse human elements brought by stakeholders—students, parents, and educators—impacted our schools.

Peterson's explanation of school culture is functional and accurately describes how the unseen human factors of a school affect the day-to-day practices and behaviors within a school. Peterson categorizes school culture into two types: positive and toxic. He describes a *positive* culture as one where "there's an informal network of heroes and heroines and an informal grapevine that passes along information about what's going on in the school . . . [a] set of values that supports professional development of teachers, a sense of responsibility for student learning, and a positive, caring atmosphere" (Cromwell, 2002, p. 15). In essence, he is saying that a positive school culture is a place where:

- Educators have an unwavering belief in the ability of all of their students to achieve success, and they pass that belief on to others in overt and covert ways.

- Educators create policies and procedures and adopt practices that support their belief in the ability of every student.

Richard DuFour, Robert Eaker, and Rebecca DuFour describe the cultural conditions necessary to create a powerful school in a way similar to Peterson (DuFour & Eaker, 1998; DuFour, DuFour, & Eaker, 2008). In order for a school to be a place that provides high levels of learning for all students regardless of student background, the staff must articulate through their behavior the beliefs that:

- All children can learn.

- All children will learn because of what we do.

DuFour, Eaker, and DuFour argue that not only must a staff hold as its fundamental belief that each child has the ability to learn, but members must also organize to utilize their resources to support that singular focus.

On the flip side, Peterson describes a *toxic* culture as one where "teacher relations are often conflictual, the staff doesn't believe in the ability of the students to succeed and a generally negative attitude prevails" (Cromwell, 2002, p. 18). That is, in a toxic culture:

- Educators believe that student success is based upon students' level of concern, attentiveness, prior knowledge, and willingness to comply with the demands of the school, and they articulate that belief in overt and covert ways.

- Educators create policies and procedures and adopt practices that support their belief in the impossibility of universal achievement.

Peterson provides an accurate description of the characteristics and function of school culture. Descriptions are helpful and provide a good starting point, but descriptions alone are inadequate to initiate transformation. I contend that in order to transform school culture, we must do more than analyze its characteristics and functionality; we must also trace its development and the educator's motivation for hanging on to paradigms that are contrary to those articulated in the public belief statements of the school or district as an organization.

Closing the Gap

Recent research has been helpful in exposing the significant power school culture wields in the functioning of schools. In fact, the American Sociological Association found that a school's level of efficacy and its collectively held expectations for student success may be the leading indicator in whether students attend post-secondary education (Jones, 2008). What is not so evident, and is perhaps even controversial, is that educators' personal belief systems may be the most powerful variables perpetuating learning gaps in our public school system. Traditional legislative mandates that focus solely on student outcomes, even when coupled with threats of embarrassment and loss of job security, may be powerless to effect change in the face of personal belief systems that perpetuate the achievement gap. In fact, this book contends that dysfunctional school cultures create systems that maintain the gap. Mary Kennedy writes, "The traditional induction to teaching encourages teachers to rely on their own prior beliefs and values for guidance and to think of their practice as a highly personal and idiosyncratic endeavor" (2005, p. 11). School culture is indeed a delicate web of past personal experience, organizational history, and interaction with the greater society; however, I contend that dysfunctional or toxic school culture is not insurmountable. As we shall see, many aspects of human behavior, social conditions, and history suggest that these types of environments can be transformed.

The goal of this book is to provide:

1. A framework for understanding how school cultures operate from a political and sociological perspective

2. Practical strategies to manipulate that culture in order to intentionally create positive atmospheres that not only tolerate change, but that seek and embrace the changes that maximize organizational effectiveness

Technical Change Versus Cultural Change

To make clear the power of school culture, I must first identify the two types of organizational change prevalent in today's schools: technical and cultural change. *Technical changes* are changes to the tools or mechanisms professionals use to do their jobs effectively. These changes within a school context refer to changes in structure, policies, or teaching tools (for example, changing from a 6-period school day to a block schedule, revising the curriculum with changes in learning standards or text material, or offering more advanced and rigorous classes, to name a few). These changes are definitely necessary to effect an improvement in student performance, but they produce very few positive results when used by people who do not believe in the intended outcome of the change.

Technical changes have become very popular in public schools, especially since the passage of NCLB. Why would educators continue to seek these surface-level changes when the United States has such a long history of initiatives that eventually overwhelm our school system's culture of low efficacy? Central leadership and site leadership have scrambled to find programs or initiatives that will be the magic bullet to fix all ailments. Terms like *research based* and *best practice* have been no match for the deeply ingrained disbelief in student ability that cripples many struggling schools. In fact, I have had the opportunity to study several schools where pessimistic faculty members are eager to prove that new strategies or programs aimed at raising student performance do not work in order to justify and solidify their hypothesis that not all students are capable of achieving excellence.

A report released by the Institute of Education Sciences (IES) revealed that the highly regarded Reading First literacy initiative, a cornerstone of President George W. Bush's education policy, has had little to no effect on student reading proficiency (Toppo, 2008). In fact, the study goes on to claim that students who received services under this initiative, which has an annual cost of over $1 billion, performed no better than students who had no exposure to this reading intervention. The evidence is clear: these types of so-called research-based strategies are no match for elements of culture that help maintain gaps in student achievement.

Cultural change is a much more difficult form of change to accomplish. It cannot be gained through force or coercion. As human beings, we do not have the ability to control the thoughts and beliefs of others, so cultural change requires something more profound. It requires leaders adept at gaining cooperation and skilled in the arts of diplomacy, salesmanship, patience, endurance, and encouragement. It takes knowledge of where a school has been and agreement about where the school should go. It requires an ability to deal with beliefs, policies, and institutions that have been established to buffer educators from change and accountability. It is a tightrope act of major proportion. But cultural change must be achieved—and it must be achieved well—if we are to prepare our current and future generations of students for an ever-changing world that is becoming more demanding each day. Substantial cultural change must precede technical change. When a school has a healthy culture, the professionals within it will seek the tools that they need to accomplish their goal of universal student achievement; they will give a school new life by overcoming the staff division that halts transformation.

CHAPTER 2

The Framework of Modern School Culture

School culture is a complex web of history, psychology, sociology, economics, and political science. To effectively diagnose and eliminate toxic school culture, we must take an honest look at the internal and external factors that create the conditions that make cultural transformation difficult.

Schools in the Era of Accountability

The accountability movement, and No Child Left Behind in particular, did not create the cultural issues confronting today's school system. But this new era has brought some deeply rooted belief systems and practices to the forefront for examination, including issues such as how we analyze, staff, and fund schools. An examination of the current environment and conditions in our schools can help us understand the myriad of paradigms that exist within the walls of our public schools and therefore help us strategize to transform the environment into a healthy one.

Who Is to Blame?

No Child Left Behind mandates the school as the responsible party when it comes to effectiveness. This is very different from the traditional belief that students and their families were primarily responsible for the effectiveness of education; educators were the experts, and schools provided students with the *opportunity* to learn. Students were expected to comply with their educators' demands to acquire knowledge. Schools believed that if parents supported the expert guidance of the teacher and encouraged their children to follow that guidance, students would succeed in school. It was not surprising, then, that all students were not academically successful, because levels of support for education were different in every household. Additionally, success or failure in school was determined solely by educators in the form of completely subjective grading scales and procedures controlled exclusively by education professionals. Parents and students had very little recourse if they felt that the system was unfair or was not an accurate appraisal of proficiency or potential.

Conversely, under NCLB, the school became exclusively accountable for student success or failure. Results of student performance on state examinations are posted in news publications for public consumption. States have developed evaluation systems for individual school districts and schools, and through this system have assigned ratings ranging from poor to excellent. The real estate industry even started using these test scores as a major factor in determining property values for homes. Schools that do not meet the mandated standards have to carry the "failing" label, even though many of them have sincerely fought to overcome barriers outside of the school's control; they have made some progress, but they have not made as much progress as the law mandates. This system of finger-pointing at schools has not motivated people to improve their practice in meaningful ways; instead, it has created anger and resentment among many educators and even more pessimism about the probability of making substantial and permanent change within schools.

I cannot blame educators for feeling unfairly blamed for all of the ills of struggling schools. I do not believe that the old paradigm of exclusively blaming students and parents is just either, but the problem of struggling schools is too complex to hold only the school system accountable for student success. In fact, the Educational Testing Service (ETS) revealed a report that validates the concerns of many educators. The report provides the following explanation for gaps in student achievement:

> The ETS researchers took four variables that are beyond the control of schools: The percentage of children living with one parent; the percentage of eighth graders absent from school

at least three times a month; the percentage of children 5 or younger whose parents read to them daily; and the percentage of eighth graders who watch five or more hours of TV a day. Using just those four variables, the researchers were able to predict each state's results on the federal eighth-grade reading test with impressive accuracy. (Winerip, 2007, p. A7)

Identifying educators as the sole cause of low student performance (or high student performance, for that matter), is not only inaccurate, but it makes the job of developing positive school culture even more difficult. Schools located in areas where risk factors for low achievement are highest are struggling to maintain a good, dedicated workforce of teachers. Negative external critiques and commentary from the public make this difficult job even more challenging and create additional problems that we must address and overcome.

Student Outcomes

The organizational mechanisms of schools were not designed to judge proficiency based upon student outcomes. A look at nearly any teacher performance evaluation proves that the school, as an organization, has concerned itself with evaluating the effort, process, compliance, and *intentions* of teachers rather than *evidence* of student learning. Decisions about lesson content, student evaluation, and classroom procedures have always been left up to each individual teacher. The leader's role was defined by his or her ability to create the conditions through which classroom teachers could exercise their autonomous endeavors. Student learning was a result of students' efforts, and, conversely, student failure was a result of students' lack of effort.

This new era of accountability has made school systems take an honest look at student outcomes and the conditions that guarantee higher achievement. District leadership has begun to demand information that more accurately and more frequently gives feedback on student performance. Consequently, teachers are challenged to analyze the effectiveness of their classroom instruction in ways that are much more objective than letter grades. What effect has this had on school culture? A focus on meeting mandates and minimum performance indicators has, in many cases, taken focus away from the individual student and his or her holistic development. Many schools are strategizing to avoid embarrassment and public humiliation for not meeting minimum student achievement goals and legislated mandates. I call this phenomenon the *compliance mentality.* This mentality has caused school systems to achieve an acceptable rating by any means necessary, including cheating on tests and excluding students with a high probability of failure on high-stakes assessments.

A Rice University study on the Texas school accountability system and its relationship to student dropout disclosed some startling revelations (Barr, 2008):

- In Texas public high schools, 135,000 youth drop out prior to graduation every year, resulting in an overall graduation rate of only 33%.

- The exit of low-achieving students made it appear as though test scores rose and that the achievement gap between white and minority students was narrowing, which increased ratings.

- There was a correlation between schools' increasing number of dropouts and their rising accountability ratings, suggesting that the accountability system allows principals to retain students deemed at risk of reducing school scores. The study found that a high proportion of students retained this way will eventually drop out.

These findings are troubling because, according to the study, "the longer such an accountability system governs schools, the more school personnel view students not as children to educate but as potential liabilities or assets for their school's performance indicators, their own careers or their school's funding" (Barr, 2008, para. 5).

In cases like this one from Texas, the accountability movement actually resulted in the students in need of the most assistance being excluded instead of helped. This certainly was not the goal of the legislation. It is important to look at student learning outcomes—but not at the expense of creating a group of disposable students for the purpose of favorable performance ratings.

Predetermination

Like any organization, schools are the sum of their parts. Educators, students, parents, and society as a whole add a component to school that is equally as challenging to deal with as the governmental laws and regulations we have just discussed. The human experience of education plays a major role in how school culture forms and ultimately how well a school operates. The unique human experiences individuals bring into the school are called *predeterminations*. There are three major forms of predetermination: *perceptual, intrinsic,* and *institutional*.

Perceptual Predetermination

Perceptual predetermination involves an educator's own socialization and the impact of that socialization on his or her practice in the classroom, including expectations for student performance. Robert Green (2005) defines teacher expectations as "inferences that teachers make about the present and future academic achievement and general classroom behavior of their students" (p. 29). Green found that these expectations for student success have a two-fold effect in the classroom:

> Teacher expectations affect student achievement primarily in two ways: first, teachers teach more material more effectively and enthusiastically to students for whom they have high expectations; second, teachers respond more favorably to students for whom high expectations are held—in a host of often subtle ways that seem to boost students' expectations for themselves. (p. 29)

So the experiences and perceptions that an educator had before he or she became an educational professional play a powerful role in how he or she perceives and serves students. Thus, the socialization of the educator is as important as his or her professional preparation. Green (2005) points out teachers generally develop positive or negative expectations around the following set of student characteristics: race, gender, social class, disability status, limited English proficiency, student history, physical attractiveness, handwriting, communication, and speech pattern. If educators have developed negative opinions about people with regard to these characteristics, students may start each class period with strikes against them.

We might assume that this problem could be eliminated if a teacher's experience or background was similar to that of his or her students. If the achievement gap is most prevalent in communities with high minority populations and homes with high poverty, perhaps we should simply hire more teachers with the same backgrounds. Unfortunately, there are not enough certified teachers to fill this demand. A 2000 study by the Applied Research Center found that there are proportionately more than twice as many African American students than certified African American teachers, and there are four times as many Hispanic students as Hispanic teachers.

In addition, upon further review of the research, we find that the race and background of the teacher does not have to be a major factor in forming student expectations. In fact, the research has found that low student expectations cross racial, ethnic, and social class lines. Teachers of similar race and class to their students are just as prone to developing low expectations. A study conducted by Ron Ferguson found that:

> Black students may not be at a disadvantage because of the "mismatch" between student and teacher race. In other words, black teachers are not always more likely to give black students more support and attention than white teachers would, because there may be other factors more powerful in guiding teacher behavior beside race like social class and generational differences. In fact, some black teachers appear to have similarly low expectations for black students as non-black teachers. (1998, p. 38)

Ferguson goes on to reveal that this mix of high and low expectations of students among teachers may help explain why poor and minority students fail to gain academic momentum and therefore fall behind students from other groups.

In a study done at five of Philadelphia's lowest performing middle schools, researchers spoke with students to get feedback from them about the kinds of teachers they needed and wanted. The students wanted teachers who were strict but fair, nice and respectful, and who took the time to explain their lessons to them clearly and effectively (Wilson & Corbett, 2001). They wanted teachers who believed in them and taught them in the ways that they learned best. These sound like very reasonable expectations. All of these characteristics are cornerstones of a healthy school culture. It is amazing that kids have figured out what they need better than the adults in the school and the so-called experts responsible for guiding these professionals.

Teacher expectations clearly play a role in how much students learn, and high expectations can be a very powerful tool if we can create conditions that allow teachers to have a favorable image of students and their ability. This involves the resocializing of those within our schools who have unfavorable expectations of student performance. We must somehow help them replace their existing belief systems with a more informed and accurate assessment of student potential. We will address this issue in chapter 6.

Intrinsic Predetermination

Intrinsic predetermination is the student's perception of his or her probability of achieving success in school. The messages students receive from their environment—the home, community, and school—can either build their confidence or work to destroy it. Students who come from homes or communities where high academic achievement is not the norm develop what Ron Ferguson calls a "self-fulfilling prophecy" (1998). The overwhelming message these students receive says that success in school is not likely. Unfortunately, for students who grow up in communities where poor academic performance is the norm, school becomes a place to hang out until you are old enough to do something else—not a place to prepare for a bright future. In fact, this message is so strong in some communities that students may feel that if they achieve in school, their peers will view them unfavorably. One study of African American students in a very prominent suburb of Cleveland, Ohio, found that many African American students were afraid of cooperating with teachers and achieving academically because of the risk of being perceived by their fellow African American peers as "acting white" (Ogbu, 2003). This type of cultural resistance to academic excellence makes the job of creating a healthy school culture even more difficult.

There is no doubt that succeeding in school takes hard work and dedication from students. No one can complete a student's assignments for him or her, and no one can take his or her exams. So students need to be immersed in an environment where they are held accountable for studying and completing their assignments, and traditionally, this responsibility has fallen on the parents. No outside influence is more powerful in a child's life than that of his or her parents. Unfortunately, students who suffer from negative intrinsic predetermination learn many of the self-defeating attitudes and behaviors from their parents. One study sought to measure the difference between the level of cognitive stimulation in poor and middle-class homes by measuring the presence of books, exposure to cultural experiences, and the amount of time parents read or participated in an academic experience with their children—factors that made up what researchers called the HOME scale. The study found that on the HOME scale of 0–100, blacks and Latinos scored 9 to 10 points lower than whites, and socioeconomically disadvantaged homes scored 12 to 15 points lower than middle-class homes. The study concluded that white students from middle-class homes experience an environment at home that is much like their surroundings at school (Jencks & Phillips, 1998).

For a school to gather the momentum necessary to transform a toxic culture into a healthy one, educators must consider students' intrinsic motivation. If students do not care to learn or feel incapable of achieving for various reasons, it will be hard to raise achievement, even if all of the adults in the school believe in them. In this journey to improvement, we must accept several realities:

1. Students are the product of their environment, and no one has the ability to choose their parents or community.

2. Student resistance is a product of their experiences. If we are to change this reality, we have to provide them with new and more productive experiences to replace the damaging experiences.

3. Children are not mature enough to understand the ramifications of academic failure; therefore, we cannot leave achievement to student interest alone. In this country, we require

individuals to be age 16 to drive an automobile, 18 to vote in an election, and 21 to drink alcohol, yet we regularly give children "licenses to fail" at a much younger age when they do not exhibit immediate interest in academics. This is not a good or reasonable practice.

Institutional Predetermination

Even though today's political climate calls for an egalitarian system of education that is dedicated to learning for all students, I contend that we have institutional barriers in place within the traditional public school system that make that goal very difficult. These policies and procedures are so ingrained within the school system that we often fail to recognize their presence and power.

This system is what Richard DuFour and Robert Eaker call a "system of sorting" (1998). They suggest that schools were never meant to serve all students; instead, they form a complex system of rules, procedures, and norms with the aim of identifying student proficiency (or lack of proficiency) and tracking students into groups ranging from to "remedial" to "gifted." Our master schedules, staffing allocations, academic policies, and support systems were built on this cognitive separation of students. This system of sorting is inherently unjust, and it depends on a certain level of polarization that will always exclude some students from the full benefit of schooling.

While traveling and consulting with schools across North America and examining course offerings at public schools, especially high schools, I have discovered that academic menus are shaped just like the bell curve. Nearly 10% of the classes are for low-performing or special education students, 80% of the classes are for the "average" or "normal" student, and 10% of the courses are made available to those identified as academically gifted. What amazes me is that regardless of location, size, or academic performance, all the schools shared this need to group students in this normal distribution.

Even though the tracking issue is most pronounced at the high school level, there is evidence that it starts much earlier. Kindergarten teachers know that students do not all start school at the same academic level. Some students show a much higher readiness level because of prekindergarten exposure to academic content and skills than students who come to school without this exposure. In the early grades, schools usually do not develop systems that physically separate students by academic ability; rather, this separation takes place in a much more informal way within the classroom. Students who show greater academic promise often get special praise, special jobs, and are generally viewed by their peers as the "teacher's pet."

By the middle grades, parents begin to become much more vocal in advocating for special classes or labels for their children that identify them as elite among students. It is not uncommon for parents to demand that their students get special attention and special classes because they are not being challenged in the regular classroom. While serving as a middle school principal for grades 6–8, I was told that we needed to create two special course sections for "advanced" students at each grade level. Each grade level consisted of 10 class sections of 30 students each, and each class section was heterogeneously grouped by past academic proficiency. I was basically instructed to isolate two sections of students, 60 students total, at each grade level and give them a label to distinguish them as "academically advanced" in comparison to the other eight class sections, or 240 students, at each grade level. It was never clear what the criteria was for this special designation; I was simply told by central office officials that parents wanted it. I became responsible for creating this pseudo-honors track that would comfortably fit into the limited honors course offerings available in our high schools.

In essence, students spend grades K–8 auditioning for their place within the bell curve. By the time students enter high school, they have already been labeled cognitively disadvantaged, cognitively average, or cognitively advanced. Schools have long operated from the perspective that their responsibility is not to ensure student attainment of predetermined skills, but rather to identify the natural talents and deficiencies of students through a standard set of assessments in order to put them in their proper place within the academic continuum. Are we serious about our goal of learning for all students if we maintain a system that thrives on formal and informal tracking?

This bell curve that we see in schools is also a microcosm of the bell curve that we experience in society. In 1994, Richard Herrnstein and Charles Murray wrote a very controversial book called *The Bell Curve: Intelligence in Class Structure in American Life.* In it, they contend that the gaps between groups that we see in our society along the lines of race, class, gender, and other variables are not socially created, but rather are the manifestation of the big difference in cognitive ability as measured through the intelligence quotient (IQ) test. They contend that low IQ, not discrimination or social inequality, is responsible for disparities in income, housing, unemployment, and family structure, among other things. They contend that America has to accept and embrace a group that they call the *cognitive elite*, those people with an IQ above 120. Herrnstein and Murray are not clear how this cognitive elite group formed, but they provide statistics to make the case that this group is most concentrated among whites and East Asian races (Herrnstein & Murray, 1994).

According to Herrnstein and Murray, we can best understand this distribution by looking at the dynamics of the bell-shaped curve of a normal statistical distribution. They contend that intelligence divides American society along that distribution; that is, the cognitive elite (very bright) make up about 10% of the population, cognitively average people make up 80% of the population ranging from bright to normal to dull, and 10% of the population make up the cognitive underclass (very dull) as measured by the IQ test. They contend that the position in which people find themselves in society depends most significantly on their natural intelligence. Herrnstein and Murray also suggest that the public school system's goal of achieving equity in student outcomes is disingenuous and that we should focus the real conversation on how to prepare each student for a "realistic" role in society based upon his or her cognitive level.

If we were to accept this argument—if success in school is merely a byproduct of students' natural cognitive talent or lack of talent—we could conclude that school reform is a waste of time. Of course, the work of researchers like Larry Lezotte and Ron Edmonds (Effective Schools) and Robert Marzano (with his mountain of empirical evidence on the effectiveness of specific teaching strategies in any environment) is enough to refute this highly suspect argument. In fact, since its publication in 1994, there have been several rebuttals to *The Bell Curve* that have proven the authors' assumptions were ill-gotten. But unfortunately their perspective on how natural intelligence impacts one's success or failure is eerily similar to the structure of today's public schools, where cognitive groupings are rigid and institutionalized. If our goal is to create a community that develops the talent of each individual student, we must take an honest look at this institutionalized system of discrimination and segregation and commit to changing it.

A War of Paradigms

The issues facing schools from outside their doors and within their walls certainly present challenges. The interaction of social, economic, parental, and political forces with the experiences and world views of educators and students creates a complex school culture that is difficult to transform.

I conducted formal and informal observations in 34 schools across the United States to try and ascertain how the staffs of these schools functioned within their school communities and how their behavior supported or hindered change that could create more favorable conditions for universal student achievement. These schools were in every geographical region of the country. Eleven were elementary schools, 14 were middle schools, and 9 were high schools. (See the appendix on page 121 for specific details about the study design.) My findings shed a new and powerful light on what we know about toxic school culture, and more importantly, on how we can overcome staff division and turn around even the most toxic cultures. I believe that if school leaders holistically understand the most important variables in unhealthy learning environments and arm themselves with strategies to uproot and replace the toxic elements, then they can be successful at creating healthy learning environments in their schools.

In my study of these 34 schools and how their educators (teachers, counselors, administrators, and support staff) interacted in the school culture and articulated their beliefs through their behavior, I found a war of belief systems. I found four distinct groups, two of which were actively engaged in a battle to make their belief system the norm of the school. Each of these groups had distinct characteristics and weapons (behaviors and tools) that they used to exercise their will. A third group found itself in the center of the battle, and a fourth group just tried to survive the school day. These four groups and their characteristics had a divisive impact on the school culture. I determined that in order to transform from a toxic to a healthy learning environment, it is essential for leaders to understand and influence change within these groups of educators within the school.

The first group I identified is the **Believers**. Believers are educators who believe in the core values that make up a healthy school culture. They believe that all of their students are capable of learning and that they have a direct impact on student success. They are actively engaged in a constant battle of ideas with another group, the Fundamentalists.

The second group I call the **Tweeners**. Tweeners are educators who are new to the school culture. Their experience can be likened to a "honeymoon period" in which they spend time trying to learn the norms and expectations of the school's culture. They end up in the middle of the war of ideas between the Believers and Fundamentalists.

The third group I identify are the **Survivors**. Fortunately, this group is not widespread in our schools. They are the small group of teachers who are "burned out"—so overwhelmed by the demands of the profession that they suffer from depression and merely survive from day to day. This group is much smaller in number than the other groups, and there is a general consensus from all groups that education is not the best profession for them.

I call the fourth group the **Fundamentalists**. Fundamentalists are staff members who are not only opposed to change, but organize to resist and thwart any change initiative. They can wield tremendous political power and are a major obstacle in implementing meaningful school reform. They actively work against the Believers.

Table 1 (page 30) shows each classification of educator and their goals. Believers believe in academic success for each student. Tweeners believe in organizational stability. Survivors are concerned with their own emotional and mental survival, and Fundamentalists want to maintain the status quo.

Table 1: The Four Types of Educators and Their Goals

Educator Classification	Organizational Goal
Believer	Academic success for each student
Tweener	Organizational stability
Survivor	Emotional and mental survival
Fundamentalist	Maintaining the status quo

In the following chapters, I will identify the distinct characteristics of each of these groups and describe how they form, behave, and interact with the school system, students, and one another to create a distinct and divided school culture.

CHAPTER 3

The Believers

We have already learned that there is a high correlation between teacher expectations and student performance. During my study of school culture, one group emerged that possessed the ability to achieve higher levels of student performance and satisfaction in the classroom as compared to their colleagues. Their actions manifested their commitment to student success. This group was composed of seasoned educators (practicing more than 3 years) who had made a decision to accept a student-centered paradigm as their primary mode of operation, regardless of outside opposition. I call this group the Believers.

I found Believers in every school I visited. Their number and level of influence varied from school to school, but their presence was definitely felt on each campus. It did not matter if the school was high or low performing; each had a set of Believers who fought in many different ways for an ideal learning environment.

A 1987 study on transformational school cultures identified 12 characteristics of powerful and positive school cultures (Butler & Dickson, 1987):

1. Collegiality

2. Experimentation

3. High expectations

4. Trust and confidence

5. Tangible support

6. Reaching out to the knowledge bases

7. Appreciation and recognition

8. Caring, celebration, and humor

9. Involvement in decision making

10. Protection of what is important

11. Honoring traditions

12. Honest, open communication

I found similar characteristics and aspirations in the Believers I studied. In their journey to establish a healthy school culture, the Believers encountered resistance. Others in the school had very different goals and worked to suppress the characteristics of positive and powerful school culture. The intensity of this clash of values became a factor in how effective Believers were within their school culture. Their intrinsic paradigm coupled with outside influences created a set of very noticeable characteristics. These characteristics included:

- High levels of intrinsic motivation

- Personal connection to the school and community

- High levels of flexibility with students

- Application of positive student pressure

- Willingness to confront opposing viewpoints

- Varied levels of pedagogical skills

The ultimate goal of Believers was success for every student academically, socially, and emotionally. They were not happy and they did not feel successful unless every child within their influence maximized his or her potential. They worked with all other willing stakeholders in multiple arenas to accomplish this goal. They had a strong presence on school improvement teams, curriculum initiatives, and voluntary committees. Change was not foreign and threatening to them; in fact, they embraced any change that they felt would improve student performance.

Intrinsic Motivation

During interviews with building principals, I asked the following question: "If you were to start an initiative that provided an extra benefit for students but required teachers to work outside of the contractual day, which staff members could you count on to participate?" Without exception, each principal's answer correlated by at least 90% with my findings: they named the same staff members whom I had already identified as Believers. Believers demonstrated a willingness to put forth more than the required effort. They made themselves available and in many cases sought opportunities to contribute to any effort that they viewed as positively affecting students.

Believers appeared to have a consistency and drive that did not depend on the influence of leadership. In the schools I observed, although teacher perception of administrator effectiveness ranged widely from "extremely low" to "exceptional," the observable characteristics of the Believers remained the same, regardless of the quality of their leadership. Many of the schools that I studied were known publicly as low performing or failing, but these labels and public perception did not seem to deter the Believers. In fact, there was no detectable difference in performance between Believers in schools labeled high performing and those labeled low performing. These indicators reveal a high level of personal commitment to education and the goals of an egalitarian educational system on the part of the Believers.

There were also several other indicators of a high level of intrinsic motivation among the Believers. One that is very telling is also very basic: work attendance. When reviewing the attendance records of the educators I observed, I found a significant disparity in days away from work between the Believers and other groups. In fact, Believers appear to understand what many researchers are just beginning to grasp: inconsistency and frequent changes in instructors greatly impact student achievement. A study by Duke University found that in North Carolina for every 10 days of absence of a 1st- or 2nd-year teacher, a student's reading and math test scores in 4th and 5th grade declined by about one-fifth the advantage of a first or second year teacher with less than 5 days absence (Keller, 2008). The study went on to find:

> Schools with high proportions of poor children suffered more from teacher absences. For instance, the poorest 25 percent of schools averaged almost one more sick day per teacher than the richest 25 percent. And schools with persistently high rates of

teacher sick and personal days were more likely to serve low-income than high-income students." (p. 11)

Believer attendance was solid in every school examined in this study, and external variables like location, ethnicity of students, socio-economic profile of the community, and personal profile of the Believer did not serve as a deterrent to solid work attendance.

Other indicators of intrinsic commitment and motivation included attendance at voluntary professional development opportunities, membership in professional organizations, and a willingness to purchase classroom materials with personal funds.

Connection to the School and Community

Another area of distinction for Believers was their life pattern. Demographic data on the participants revealed a clear pattern of home ownership within reasonable proximity to the school. Only 10% of the Believers in this study rented their residence or had an unstable housing situation. The home ownership variable reveals that the Believers made a conscious decision to build their lives in close proximity to their work environment, which indicates that they plan to continue their employment and participation at their school for some time to come.

Many of the Believers I interviewed indicated that they met their spouse in the community in which they live and work and that their children either attended the district of their employment or a neighboring district. Their religious and civic alliances were also built in close proximity to their home and work environments, further solidifying their ties to the school community.

This commitment to their profession and individual schools brought Believers a sense of stability and appeared to shape their relationships with students in a positive way; they shared a community with them. During classroom observations, students would regularly talk about seeing their teacher at the grocery store or at church. This sense of familiarity seemed to produce a positive bond between students and educators.

Flexibility

Of all the characteristics of Believers, none was more striking than the high level of flexibility they demonstrated. While other educators were very strict with school rules, grading procedures, seating arrangements, and other similar issues, Believers sought to individualize their responses to students instead of adopting a rigid approach to student relations. It was clear that the main goal of the Believers—student success—motivated their desire to be flexible. In one seventh-grade science classroom I observed, students lined up at the teacher's desk to turn in a science project. The class had been working on the project for over 6 weeks, and their grades on the project would constitute more than 50% of their final grades for the marking period. As students lined up, one young lady still sat with her arms folded on her desk and her head resting on her arms. When she finally lifted her head, it was apparent she had been crying. After all the projects had been turned in, the teacher, a Believer, noticed the student's posture, tapped her, and asked the student to follow her into the hall so that they could talk. When they returned, the expression on the student's face and her entire disposition had changed dramatically. She was smiling, and the anxiety she displayed earlier seemed to have dissipated.

After the students were released from class, I approached the teacher to inquire about her actions in the hall and the source of the student's anxiety. The teacher explained that this student was very conscientious and had never missed a deadline for turning in an assignment. She went on to explain that the student's parents were going through a painful divorce, and the combativeness of her parents sometimes caused her to be displaced with relatives. The previous evening, the teacher explained, the student's father was intoxicated and tried to force his way into their home. Her mother called the police, and her father was arrested. Consequently, the student spent the evening at her aunt's home. Her science project was at her dad's apartment, and the student did not know if she could return to get it any time soon. The teacher extended the deadline for the student, and she informed her that she would share the details of her situation with the principal so they could contact the father to see if he would be willing to drop the project off at school. The teacher followed through with his promise, and before the day was over, the girl's grandfather delivered her project to the school.

In this situation, the teacher chose to talk to the student before drawing a conclusion about her anxiety and penalizing her for the lateness of the very important assignment. When I asked the teacher about her flexible and personalized approach to the situation, she replied, "I want these kids to learn and love science. I do not care about rules or deadlines. I want to spark something special in my students, and if bending a little does the trick, that is a small price to pay."

Believers also showed flexibility in their classroom management and in their interpretation of the student code of conduct. When reviewing school discipline data, Believers wrote formal discipline referrals to the office at nearly 30% the rate of Fundamentalists. Was it that the Believers did not encounter student discipline issues? The answer is no; they, too, encountered difficult students. What differed were the methods they used to manage discipline incidents. These methods were rooted in intentions that differed significantly from those of other groups in the school.

Believers generally had high expectations for student conduct, but they chose to use nonpunitive measures more often than punitive measures. When behavior issues arose, they relied heavily on student loyalty, which they gained through positive personal relationships. Students seemed to lament the fact that they disappointed an advocate instead of rejoicing over whatever personal pleasure that gained through the conduct violation.

Believers used observable classroom management techniques at a much higher rate than other groups within the school. Many of these techniques were informal and private. A significant number of Believers had a "look" that communicated seriousness to a student who was violating a rule. This had an immediate impact on the student that other teachers, even after writing disciplinary referrals and threatening punishment, could not achieve. The authors of *Listening to Urban Kids: School Reform and the Teachers They Want* found that the children they studied in urban Philadelphia schools really admired and respected teachers who "stayed on them" and "made them be successful" (Wilson &

Corbett, 2001). Students in these schools had a very low level of respect for teachers who wrote a lot of referrals; they considered them to be "weak" and "scared" (p. 71). Students in the Believers' classrooms displayed a high level of respect for their teachers. They knew these teachers believed strongly in students' ability to not only achieve academically, but also behaviorally. And they knew their teachers understood that they would make mistakes at times. There was an understanding that most issues would be resolved in the classroom, and the main office was reserved for serious issues or severe problems.

Positive Pressure

Believers do not want to see any student fail. This desire produces a very observable characteristic called positive pressure. Positive pressure is a collection of unrelenting responses to student underperformance and apathy. The teacher simply does not allow the student to fail. In the classrooms of Believers I observed, it was apparent that to students, failure was not a possibility. Even students who were not performing well in other classes met at least minimum learning standards in Believers' classrooms.

Strategies for positive pressure took many forms, including calling parents, moving a student's seat closer to the teacher, detaining students from lunch or recess socialization, providing positive incentives, and requiring after-school tutoring, to name a few. If one strategy did not produce the breakthrough that the Believer expected, he or she tried a new one and repeated this process until the student met the classroom academic and behavioral expectations. Some Believers used a stoic and very strict approach in their pressure, and others took a motivational approach similar to a football coach firing the team up before the biggest game of the season. Their methods varied, but the end result consistently indicated that the student understood that failure was not an option in the classroom and that resistance only brought on a new wave of pressure.

It was very apparent that Believers felt every student was capable of learning the assigned curriculum. Believers did not have different performance expectations for each student. The evidence is very clear that varying student expectations based upon unscientific observation has a real effect on student performance:

> In his 1983 review of the teacher expectations research, Jerry Brophy estimated that five to ten percent of the variance in student performance is attributable to differential treatment accorded them based on their teachers' differential expectations of them. Various other researchers have accepted and quoted this estimate. Five to ten percent is hardly the epidemic of mistreatment and negative outcomes perceived by some educators and members of the general public, but it is significant enough, particularly when compounded through year after year of schooling, to warrant concern. (Cotton, 1989, p. 11)

This unwavering expectation of universal student achievement was the driving force behind all of the positive pressure.

In a ninth-grade science class, a young man entered the classroom, put his head on the desk, and withdrew from class participation before the class had even officially begun. His teacher approached him and whispered in his ear. I guessed that he was giving the student gentle verbal encouragement to participate with the class. The student did not respond. About 2 minutes later, the teacher approached the student again and told the whole class how much he really wanted the disinterested student to come to the front and help him demonstrate an experiment. This attempt caused the student to lift his head for a moment and make eye contact with the teacher, but he still did not speak or move to participate. On the third attempt, the teacher stated to the class that the disinterested student was a scientific whiz kid and his great performance during last week's football game proved how well he solved problems, and that he was best qualified to demonstrate this experiment. The teacher expressed to the class that "the best" was the only acceptable option in his class and that the class would not continue until the disinterested student assisted with the demonstration. This caused many of the more involved and interested students to verbally coerce the student into participating. As he approached the teacher, the student mumbled his displeasure, but the peer pressure had cracked his aloof disposition, and he complied with the teacher's command to participate for the rest of the class period.

After the class ended, I asked the teacher how often he used similar techniques with this student. He told me about once per week, but during the first 3 weeks of school he had to use them daily. The student was currently earning a C in his class, and he had never before passed a science class since entering secondary school. The teacher further explained that failure is not allowed in his class and that rule is nonnegotiable. He expressed that he would use every available means to enforce this rule.

Willingness to Confront

Many of the attributes of Believers—such as high expectations for student behavior and achievement, effective connection with students, patience, and flexibility—reflect best practice as supported by the research on improving student performance. It would seem, then, that Believers would aggressively recruit others to these ideas; however, this was not the case in the classrooms I studied. In fact, Believers tended to speak out and challenge others only when something overtly intolerant was exhibited. Believers, as a whole, appeared to be passive and permissive of others where issues of inequity, low student expectations, and roadblocks to school reform were concerned, except in extreme cases.

In one staff meeting I observed in a rural middle school, the principal delivered a presentation on the latest student test results from their state's standardized test. The news was not good. Not only did student performance not improve, it actually got worse. As the meeting went on, it was apparent that all were displeased they had missed their federal achievement goal of adequate yearly progress (AYP) for the third straight year. One of the staff members raised his hand as the principal finished explaining all of the details of the assessment results and said, "We never had this problem before they built that trailer park around the corner." Immediately, two Believers scolded him for his comments. I only observed Believers speaking out or challenging viewpoints in similar extreme circumstances. When their peers exhibited similar beliefs through much more subtle means, such as in casual comments about student potential, general complaints about school or district function, or consistent pessimism about the school-improvement process, Believers were silent. They appeared to be content to work with their students and control their own spheres of influence instead of actively engaging their colleagues in philosophical debates about what they felt was best for students.

If schools are going to effectively create positive and productive cultures, the Believers simply have to become more active and aware of the day-to-day assaults on the very belief system to which they adhere. They have strong cases for their stance: research and ethics support their goal of success for every student. If Believers would simply engage in intellectual discourse on a regular and consistent basis, they might discover that they could change school culture for the better beyond their own spheres.

Pedagogical Skill

The Believers' paradigm was very consistent: all students must be successful. But there were huge variances in the level of teaching skill Believers exhibited. In many cases, I observed Believers who not only held to the principle that all students can learn, but they employed teaching methodologies that best promoted the achievement of that goal. In these classrooms, I observed many instances of effective use of instructional technology, cooperative learning activities, differentiation for student learning style, and ongoing formative assessment with immediate feedback for students. These methods, coupled with the teacher's belief systems, made Believers' classrooms havens for student performance.

Unfortunately, in many other classrooms, I observed similar paradigms with pedagogy that perpetuated gaps in student achievement. Simply put, many Believers wanted all of their children to learn at high levels, but they did not know how to make that desire a reality. In many cases, I observed all of the character attributes of a Believer coupled with methods like silent reading, hour-long lectures, photocopied worksheets, and low-level question-and-answer sessions. It was apparent that the teachers who used these methods were affected by their students' lack of growth, but they were clueless to the fact that their methodology was the key variable in that lack of growth.

In order to close the achievement gap, we need to do more than just believe in our students; we need to properly instruct and guide them. Our field has a wealth of available research on the most effective teaching methods for each student enrolled in our public school system. Educators who adopt egalitarian idealism as the center of their educational paradigm must cultivate professionalism as well. In order to achieve an end, a person must have conviction, but that conviction must be buttressed with skill.

A Unifying Force

Believers display the qualities and value the paradigms that unite staff members and make a positive school culture. Their core beliefs are in alignment with the stated mission of schools: success for every student. They have high expectations for student achievement, and they are willing to embrace strategies that improve their performance. They have made a commitment, not only to the field, but also to the communities that they serve. If schools are to transform their cultures into fertile ground for positive experimentation and student nurturing, they must increase their population of Believers, and their Believers must become more vocal members of the school community.

CHAPTER 4

The Tweeners

A Tweener is anyone who is new to a particular culture. The most common Tweeners in the schools I observed were new educators who had recently graduated from college and were experiencing their first teaching jobs, and, less frequently, educators who had chosen teaching as a second career. I call brand-new educators *Level One Tweeners;* they made up 91% of the educators identified in the Tweener category in this study. But an experienced educator who moves into a new school, district, or job categorization is also a Tweener. I refer to these educators as *Level Two Tweeners;* because their introduction and socialization into their new environment does not have nearly the impact on school culture as the Level Ones, they are not the focus of this chapter.

My study revealed that a new educator, a Level One Tweener, has an introductory period of 2 to 4 years. A Level Two Tweener (one who changes work environments within the field of education) has a shorter introductory period of 1 to 2 years. This introductory period is unpredictable. What happens then can shape the career of these educators and the school environments in which they work. Therefore, the primary goal of a Tweener is to find stability within the organization and understand how he or she fits within the cultural and political goals of the organization.

A Loose Connection

One of the very easily observable characteristics of the Tweeners, especially the first-time educators, was their very loose connection with the school and community. Simply put, they did not have a lot at stake within the organization. Their connection was created by their employment contract or employment agreement, and that relationship could be broken easily.

Unlike the Believers, the Tweeners had a very low level of home ownership. Of the Tweeners studied, 92% identified themselves as renters, and more than 70% had at least one roommate who was not a relative. This is significant because home ownership creates a natural bond with a city or region. It is a major step in establishing roots. This characteristic makes the Tweeners huge flight risks. They have not made the financial commitments that symbolize stability and longevity.

Because the vast majority of Level One Tweeners are recent college graduates, it should not be surprising that the median age was 24. It should also not be surprising that only 9% had children and 18% were married. These two factors also create bonds to a city or a region that could promote longevity within the school system.

Tweeners' loose coupling with the organization makes leaving a viable choice at all times. The bonds that prevent mobility are simply not present for them. If schools are going to develop their cultures, they must take this fact into serious consideration. Administrators must do more than simply hire people with attractive resumes and hope that they stay and become positive contributors to the staff.

School leaders can strengthen these loose bonds by intentionally creating strong bonds in other areas. As I interviewed Tweeners, I asked them about their personal lives, and they were more than happy to share details with me. Many expressed affinity for sports, the arts, religion, community service, and a host of other interests. When I asked if their administrators had inquired about their personal interests, I heard a nearly unanimous "no." The personal interests of Tweeners can be a powerful link in the quest to retain these new educators in our schools. Intentionally placing these new professionals in key positions within our schools that connect with their areas of personal interest can create a bond with the school that may not occur otherwise. These bonds help Tweeners navigate the sometimes-tumultuous early years in the classroom and create the positive experiences necessary for them to align their paradigms with those of the Believers.

Strengthening the bond of Tweeners is absolutely crucial to the development of positive school culture. A recent study indicated that 50% of new teachers who enter the educational profession leave the field before their 5th year in the classroom; in urban areas, that number escalates to nearly 70% (Hunt, 2003). How can schools improve if they lose half of their new practitioners before their 5th year of practice? This creates constant turnover in the classroom, which studies have indicated hinders the academic progress of students (Barnes, Schaefer, & Crowe, 2007).

More importantly, schools simply cannot gather the momentum necessary to create change over the long term because they lack *organizational memory*—the momentum carried from year to year by an organization's members. This phenomenon is very observable in the world of team sports. Teams that build a core group of players who grow and develop together and take positive steps toward winning a championship carry the goals and norms of the team with them from year to year. An athlete who joins that team is quickly introduced to the norms, values, and goals of that team, and key members of the team force compliance with their influence. On the flip side, if a team's roster of athletes and coaches changes from year to year and no clear nucleus is established, that team usually flounders and struggles to search for an identity. Consequently, victories become rare as the team grows more and more unstable. Schools are no different. Unless the school achieves positive stability through a large coalition of its members, it is incapable of sustaining growth over time. If membership constantly turns over, training and professional initiatives have no long-term effectiveness. School districts that are serious about growth and reform must be proactive in their plans to strengthen the bond between the school and the Tweener.

An Enthusiastic Nature

Tweeners are enthusiastic about what they can contribute to their students, school, community, and nation through their service in the classroom. Interviews with new teachers clearly reveal that they do not become educators because they seek financial wealth. A recent report on motivating and retaining new teachers by the National Education

Association (NEA) also found that new teachers seek the profession for intrinsic satisfaction as opposed to financial gain (Kopkowski, 2008). Indeed, teachers' starting salaries are much lower than many other professions.

The Tweeners I studied cited many reasons for their career choice. Many said that they were inspired by a teacher during their own K–12 schooling experience and they wanted to provide that same inspiration for others. Nearly 20% of those interviewed indicated that at least one of their parents was an educator and he or she wanted to follow their career path. Several Tweeners described some religious conviction that called them into service through the classroom. A significant number of Tweeners simply indicated that they wanted to serve humanity and "give back" to society. The reasons may have varied, but it was clear that Tweeners chose the field of education because they felt they could make a positive impact on society.

This willingness to serve takes many forms in the beginning stages of a teaching career. Tweeners tried to immerse themselves in their new culture by participating in voluntary committees, attending staff social functions, and arriving at the school site early and leaving late. Tweeners, especially in the beginning stages, seized every opportunity to learn about their new environment.

This enthusiasm was evident in the classroom as well, especially when it came to the aesthetic quality of the classroom, which reflected a focus on theme and decoration and what Tweeners learned during their time in college methods courses. The classroom of the typical Tweener seemed to be a monument to his or her subject matter and the students he or she served. Additionally, there was very clear evidence of recent research-based pedagogical methods, which also directly reflected their recent status as college students. Lessons that took into account student learning style or multiple intelligence research were not uncommon. The Tweeners were typically not afraid to experiment and try a wide variety of methods in the classroom.

Tweeners also appeared to be very enthusiastic about achieving universal academic proficiency within their classrooms. When asked about barriers to learning like poverty, minimal parental involvement, and attendance, the typical Tweener believed that he or she could over-come one or all of these obstacles. They were honest enough to admit that they did not know exactly how to achieve this reality, but they felt that with hard work and perseverance, they and their students could overcome these factors. In essence, they believed that all of their students could learn at high levels, but they were not quite sure how to accomplish that end.

The "Honeymoon Period" and Compliance

Approaching any new situation can cause a person to become cautious and reluctant to reveal their faults—both perceived and real—to others. Tweeners are no different. Because they are new to the school culture, they often display reluctance to being viewed unfavorably by their new peers. This is a natural phenomenon. There is no person that the Tweener wants to impress more than his or her supervisor, primarily the school principal. This person has the power to determine whether or not the new educator continues his or her employment with the school or district, and in some cases whether he or she stays in the field. School administrators have the tremendous power of evaluation, which can be intimidating—especially to someone who is simply trying to find comfort and stability within an organization. Tweeners in the study generally displayed a high level of reverence—sometimes bordering on fear—for their school and district supervisors.

This fear and uncertainty caused an observable obsession among Tweeners for pleasing a supervisor, primarily through compliance with directives. Whenever Tweeners were given orders, they complied. In the mind of a Tweener, missing a deadline or ignoring a directive could mean displeasing the principal and in turn threaten their livelihood within the profession. Tweeners hoped that compliance with directives would articulate to administrators that they were team players, and that in return administrators would reward them with favorable evaluations.

During my interviews, I asked principals their opinions of certain teachers. I knew how I had categorized those teachers, but the principals did not. Time after time, the administrator identified the Tweener teacher as a "good teacher." When I probed and asked for

evidence of proficiency, the principals expressed that these good teachers were compliant and cooperative, had high levels of collegiality, and
were politically neutral. There was rarely any evidence given relating
to their proficiency in the most important aspect of the schooling:
student learning. Principals were pleased that the Tweeners followed
directions and complied with mandates—but are these the criteria for
good professional practice in today's environment? Today's school leaders have to be concerned with issues far more important than management tasks and compliance with mandates. An overwhelming body
of evidence proves that highly effective schools have school leaders
who are strong *instructional* leaders (Maccoby, 2008). These leaders are
involved in critical decisions about what students learn and how students are assessed, and they help develop support systems that ensure
high levels of learning for all students. This type of leader is especially
necessary in the current era of academic accountability.

This very surface-level look at teacher performance blinded some
administrators to hidden problems. Though Tweeners displayed an
enthusiastic disposition in public, many of them suffered from the
trials of learning to master their craft. Foundational tasks and issues
such as classroom management, implementation of curriculum,
administrative paperwork, and the fast pace of school make the first
few years of teaching difficult (Allen, 2005). How could a Tweener
balance the need to please the administrator and at the same time seek
support for the many struggles experienced within the first few years
in the profession? The balance is very difficult to strike. Administrators
often assume everything is running smoothly because of the Tweeners'
high level of compliance and sunny disposition, but the teacher may be
experiencing significant difficulty and trials. This causes some Tweeners,
especially the ones who struggle severely in their first few years in the
profession, to live in two worlds: a private world of struggle and doubt,
and a public world of false enthusiasm and positivity. These two worlds
are on a collision course to what I call the *moment of truth*.

The moment of truth is the very critical moment when an educator questions his or her likelihood of continuing in the field. Any
experienced educator remembers that moment well and the conditions
that caused it. The reasons can vary from an explosive confrontation

with parents to an unresponsive student who refuses to comply with classroom rules and regulations. No matter what the circumstance, this very painful moment is significant in the career of an educator. It is the first time the educator seriously questions whether he or she will continue or consider other career options. I am sure there are similar moments in any career, but for educators, who very often choose education in order to serve the common good, this moment can be especially painful.

In one very vivid example, I observed a young middle school science teacher who appeared to have all of the necessary attributes to evolve into being a very solid educator. Upon my initial observations, she displayed the trademark enthusiasm and willingness to serve that are typical of a Tweener. I observed her in her classroom, which showed all the evidence of her recent college courses and the teaching methods she used with her students.

I returned to the same school the following fall, nearly a year later, and her entire disposition had changed. She appeared personally and professionally withdrawn, combative with students, and generally pessimistic about the direction of the school. I approached her principal after the second observation and inquired about the drastic change in her behavior. He informed me that she had a very traumatic experience in the middle of the previous school year from which she had not yet recovered. She had a disagreement with a student about a grade the student received on a very important classroom project. After being unable to convince the teacher that her grade should be changed, the student went to the restroom to call her mother from her cell phone. The student returned to class, and the teacher continued to teach. Shortly after the student returned to class, her mother appeared in the classroom and confronted the teacher, hurling profanity and insulting comments until the teacher began to cry. Some of the students showed support for their teacher, while others laughed at her misfortune. This became her crucial moment of truth.

A critical event such as this in the career of a Tweener signifies prime recruitment time for Fundamentalists (discussed in detail in chapter 6). Fundamentalists displayed a consistent pattern of refraining from heavily influencing Tweeners until they had personally experienced an unexpected disruption to their development. This technique proved to be very savvy and effective. Fundamentalists greatly increased their likelihood of success at selling their political stance while the Tweener was in a weak or vulnerable moment. The strategy was to teach the Tweener how to survive and maintain sanity by isolating themselves from the other parts or members of the school. They convinced the Tweener that belonging to the brotherhood of educators who had also been through a critical experience and survived was essential to longevity in the field. Their words and outward showing of empathy provided the Tweener with a sense of comfort, and later the Tweener started to share many more job frustrations, causing the new educator to eventually become a Fundamentalist. I observed this pattern repeatedly in many different schools and circumstances.

How could this have been avoided? First of all, site and district administrators must realize that new educators will struggle in the early phases of practice. Tweeners need to know that those in leadership positions support them and are not only willing to listen to their struggles, but also will be a partner in resolving those struggles. Second, administrators must establish and institutionalize proper and ongoing mentorship. The Tweener needs to be connected with a stellar example of professionalism and have access to that mentor on a regular basis. Third, school leadership must methodically work to connect the new educator to the school community. This can be done effectively through making an immediate and positive connection with the Tweener—by taking advantage of the gifts and talents he or she brings to the school. This personal connection will increase the likelihood that the new educator will have a vested interest in the school and that negative experiences will be counteracted with a series of positive experiences to help them weather the storm of the moment of truth.

Why Are Tweeners So Important?

If public schools are to improve, the Tweeners must be secured and vested in the long-term future of our system. Every year, many of our best and brightest college students graduate and enter the ranks of the teaching profession. The problem is that they do not stay. One-third of teachers leave in the first 3 years of practice, and nearly half leave before they reach year 5 in the profession—a number that has approached 70% in schools that are predominately poor and populated with minority students (Hunt, 2003).

A report by the National Education Association (NEA) describes the problem like this:

> Their departure [new teachers] through what researchers call the "revolving door" that's spinning ever faster . . . costs roughly $7 billion a year, as districts and states recruit, hire, and try to retain new teachers. "There is this idea that we can solve the teaching shortage with recruitment," says commission President Tom Carroll. "What we have is a retention crisis." Likening it to continually dumping sand into a bucket with holes in the bottom, Carroll says, "as fast as [the districts] are moving teachers into schools, they're leaving." (Kopkowski, 2008, p. 2)

If schools, especially those serving the lowest achieving groups, fail to retain new practitioners, the progress that we hope to achieve in public schools is highly unlikely and probably impossible to achieve. If the poorest and neediest students are consistently guided by novice professionals who never evolve into proficient instructors, they will constantly be behind.

Tweeners are important for two major reasons: first, as noted in the previous chapter, a school cannot gain momentum if it lacks organizational memory. Members of an organization who are connected to a long-term plan for improvement and participate in that improvement incrementally over time carry with them the experiences, training, and expertise necessary to make that long-term vision a reality. This type of long-range continuity is not possible if the members of an organization consistently change and initiatives have to be revamped or scrapped because knowledge and experience are lost through a revolving door. New members then enter the organization clueless about the past attempts to improve the organization and the organizational vision. Organizations with no memory simply survive; they never reach a point where they can thrive. America's schools cannot make long-term progress if they replace 50% of their professional staff every 5 years.

Tweeners are also important to the evolution of a school and its culture because they present the best opportunity for the growth of the Believers. Administrators can look at schools with a very high number of inexperienced teachers as either a crisis or an opportunity. We must remember that Tweeners are trying to find stability and meaning; they are blank slates. Administrators who provide these new professionals with proper support can fill that slate with good experiences and drastically change the culture of the school.

The National Staff Development Council (NSDC) agrees, and they make the following recommendations:

> Teachers—even those in the most demanding settings—are far more likely to remain in their positions when they feel supported by administrators, have strong bonds of connection to colleagues, and are aggressively pursuing a collective vision for student learning about which they feel passion and commitment. Teachers' connections to the profession and to their schools are also strengthened when they feel they possess the content knowledge, instructional skills, and technological tools to meet the challenges of standards-based education in increasingly diverse classrooms. (Sparks, 2002, p. 4)

The recommendations of the National Commission on Teaching and America's Future (NCTAF) are consistent with those of NSDC. In their report *No Dream Denied: A Pledge to American Children* (2003), they note that the era of solo teaching in isolated classrooms is over:

> Good teaching thrives in a supportive learning environment created by teachers and school leaders who work together to improve learning—in short, quality teaching requires strong, professional learning communities. Collegial interchange, not isolation, must become the norm for teachers. (p. 17)

Leaving Nothing to Chance

The evidence is clear: school leaders cannot leave new teacher development to chance. Leaders must be proactive and put time and resources behind the support and development of Tweeners. By doing this, we can methodically create the positive school cultures we need for our schools to universally evolve into high-performing organizations. The future of our schools is in jeopardy if we cannot create a system that protects and grooms our Tweeners into the type of educators that will achieve longevity in the field and adopt the types of philosophies and practices that increase student learning. Paying close attention to their needs and developing systems of support will go a long way in reducing the turnover rate. Socializing them in the progressive and visionary goals of public school will ensure that Tweeners do more than stay in the profession; it will ensure their effectiveness for years to come.

CHAPTER 5

The Survivors

During the course of this study, a small but important group of teachers emerged. This group was not large in number, and in most cases, leaders responded appropriately to their needs. I call this group the Survivors. A Survivor is an educator who has completely given up on practicing effective instruction and has focused his or her energy on a new mission: survival until the end of the school year—and in some cases, the end of the school day. The Survivors made up less than 2% of the educators observed in this study, but if gone unchecked, they can have an absolutely devastating impact on their students' chances of receiving a quality education.

A comprehensive study conducted at the University of Tennessee showed that students assigned to ineffective teachers continue to show the effects of such teachers even when those students are subsequently assigned to very effective teachers (Sanders & Rivers, 1996). The residual effects of both very effective and ineffective teachers are measurable 2 years later, regardless of the effectiveness of teachers in later grades. The same study also found that students who have three effective teachers or three ineffective teachers in a row have vastly different achievement levels. Because of differences in teacher effectiveness, students whose achievement levels were similar in mathematics at the beginning of third grade scored 50 percentile points apart on fifth-grade achievement tests just 3 years later. Poor and ineffective instruction can completely undermine the fundamental mission of the school. This is why leaders must remove teachers who have become burnt out or depressed from the classroom and address their issues. It is what is best for the student as well as the teacher.

Flight Response

When human beings face stress that becomes overwhelming, they psychologically retreat to a safer place, away from the overwhelming stress. The field of education is very demanding, and practitioners face many challenges both in and outside of the classroom. These challenges include classroom organization, lesson planning, student evaluation, discipline, parent and community relations, and administrative requirements. All of these responsibilities can cause some moments of extreme stress for even the most prepared and experienced educators.

A recent study made a distinction between workplace stress and what has been categorized as "burnout." According to the study, "workplace burnout isn't the same as workplace stress. When you're stressed, you care too much, but when you're burned out, you don't see any hope of improvement"(Smith, Jaffe-Gill, Segal, & Segal, 2007, p. 2). Nearly everyone experiences workplace stress, but people who have burnout have become shells of their former selves; the psychological flight response has been triggered, and they descend into depression.

A study conducted by Teri McCarthy-Wood and Chris Wood (2002) traced the development of teacher burnout:

> When a potentially threatening event is encountered, a reflexive, cognitive balancing act ensues, weighing the perceived demands of the event against one's perceived ability to deal with them. Events perceived as potential threats trigger the stress response, a series of physiological and psychological changes that occur when coping capacities are seriously challenged. The most typical trigger to the stress response is the perception that ones' coping resources are inadequate for handling life demands. . . . Teacher stress may be seen as the perception of an imbalance between demands at school and the resources teachers have for coping with them. Symptoms of stress in teachers can include anxiety and frustration, impaired performance, and ruptured interpersonal relationships at work and home. (pp. 109–110)

The balancing act that teachers have to perform is very real. Unfortunately, the consequences of an inability to handle this balancing act of demands from students, parents, colleagues, and administration can adversely affect both a person's psychological and physical well being. Survivors should not be ridiculed or demeaned; their condition is real and they require help.

Student Bargaining

What became immediately apparent to me in this study was that the Survivors were not in control of their own emotions, which made it difficult for them to manage the behavior of others, particularly students. Students are adept at quickly identifying the teachers who have reached this level of withdrawal, and they take advantage of the situation.

With life at work spiraling out of control, it is surprising that Survivors can actually manage to make it from day to day and year to year. They do so by engaging in tacit, informal bargaining with their students. The Survivor extends an olive branch to students and offers them the opportunity to bargain for the conditions that would allow for a peaceful coexistence. In a nutshell, Survivors want to know what it will take for students to agree to leave them alone.

Students, of course, seize this opportunity to gain privileges that they know would never be allowed in other classes. I witnessed some of the spoils of their shrewd bargaining:

- Use of banned electronic items such as music devices and video games

- Access to the computer for personal purposes

- Access to nonacademic television and video programs

- The opportunity to bring food and beverages into the classroom

- Receipt of favorable grades in exchange for compliance with the teacher

As long as students are happy and compliant, this system remains intact. The students get what they want, and the teacher gets what he or she wants. As long as this agreement is in place, the class appears to an unsuspecting supervisor as orderly and harmonious. But this system tends to break down on a regular basis. Some students become increasingly demanding, and those concerned with achievement become frustrated with the lack of learning opportunities and begin to involve their parents. When this happened during my study, the administration was forced to act. We will examine their response in the latter part of this chapter.

Pedagogical Characteristics

Survivors' psychological withdrawal causes many observable characteristics. The Survivors carry no political agenda. Their sole purpose is to make it to the end of each school day with their sanity intact. They do not interact much with other educators, and when they do, the conversation is usually of a personal nature. "Shop talk" is not something Survivors value or engage in.

The most noticeable and damaging characteristic of a Survivor is the absence of good professional practice. In fact, many of the Survivors I observed showed no evidence of professional practice or even the desire to use good professional practices. I regularly observed the following teaching techniques from Survivors:

- Frequent use of video as a primary teaching tool
- Frequent use of the computer lab for nonacademic reasons
- Frequent use of worksheets as "busy work" to fill time
- Frequent granting of free time as a reward for behavioral cooperation

The Survivors I observed were not very well respected among their peers. All of the stakeholders in the organization agreed that the Survivors were not good for the school and condemned their practices universally. Many educators felt sympathy for them, but there was consensus that Survivors did not belong in the classroom in their current state of mind.

Organizational Response

When professionals, especially those responsible for the well being of children, reach a point where they spiral into a pit of depression that they cannot dig themselves out of, the organization must respond—and respond swiftly. The state of the Survivor cannot be ignored or easily fixed. The best and only real solution is to remove the Survivor from the conditions that caused the depression until he or she can get proper treatment (Haberman, 2005). Wishful thinking or turning a blind eye will not solve the problem, and leaving Survivors in the environment that caused their psychological breakdown can only make matters worse.

In the cases I observed, the administration generally used the following methods to deal with Survivors:

- Reassigned the teacher to a less challenging teaching assignment

- Worked with officials to have the teacher transferred to another school within the district with the hope that a change in environment might be invigorating

- Counseled the teacher into retirement, if that option was available

- Ignored the symptoms and responded harshly to the disruptive students in an attempt to force them to cooperate with the teacher

- Dealt strictly with the professional behavior without consideration for the cause and responded harshly to the teacher through a series of punitive measures for nonperformance

- Sought the teacher's removal through termination or some form of medical leave

Dealing With Stress and Pressure

The stress that comes with working in schools is very real. Pressure from all sides—administration, colleagues, students and their families, the community at large, the government, and a teacher's responsibilities at home—can cause anyone to have a bad day from time to time. But when these pressures become overwhelming, they can do real physical and psychological damage. When teachers burn out and succumb to the daily stress, neither they nor their students benefit. They become locked in a nonproductive, educationally stagnant environment, and swift action and intervention by those in authority is necessary.

The good news is that many school leaders do act to reduce the effects Survivors have on students. All the administrators I observed in my study acted—they did not turn their heads and pretend that the problem did not exist. In all but one case, the Survivor was removed from the situation, and as result the conditions of the classroom drastically and instantly improved. In several cases, the district provided psychological treatment and paid employment leave through its insurance carrier, and the educators had an opportunity to return if cleared by the treating physician. When these conditions manifest themselves, the best we can hope to do is to shield the educator and the students from further damage.

CHAPTER 6

The Fundamentalists

Of the four types of educators I observed in schools and class-rooms during my study, the two with the most influence and importance to school culture are the Believers and the Fundamentalists. A Fundamentalist is an experienced educator who believes that there is one pure and undisputable way to practice: the traditional model of schooling. They are the vanguards of tradition and the protectors of the status quo. They are relentless in their attempts to discourage change and protect a system that has allowed them to function and thrive, and they organize to protect this traditional way of practice. Their experiences have led them to believe that the traditional model of schooling is the best and purest model of schooling. It is the system that was used to educate them, and it is the system they were socialized into when they became new professionals. They have learned the rules of that system, and they understand how it functions and how to excel within it. They view change itself as an enemy; therefore, anyone who challenges the system is a threat to the system and a threat to the Fundamentalists. They are the most aggressive and vocal combatants in this war of ideology.

The dictionary defines *fundamentalism* as a movement or attitude stressing strict and literal adherence to a set of basic principles, and a *fundamentalist* as one with a strong adherence to a basic set of beliefs even in the face of criticism or unpopularity (Merriam-Webster, 2008). Even though the term *fundamentalist* is often used in the religious arena, it clearly applies to people and belief systems outside of religion.

Any school leader interested in producing a healthy school culture must understand the Fundamentalists and how they operate. They pose the biggest threat to change and improvement in our school system. Albert Einstein is quoted as saying that insanity is defined as "doing the same thing over and over again and expecting a different result" (Tangredi, 2005, p. 1). If our schools are going to improve student learning, they must embrace strategies that are radically different from those we have embraced in the past. An organization that does not change and evolve does not improve. An organization that does not improve is doomed to fail. Fundamentalists do not intend to destroy or ruin schools. Quite the contrary: They believe their paradigm is correct, that standing up for what they believe in is pure and fundamental, and that they will indeed save the institution. But their stance causes a dilemma. Leaders are being pushed to make meaningful and substantive change in schools, which means that some practices and values will have to change. This immediately puts leaders at odds with Fundamentalists who are zealous about maintaining the status quo and tradition.

Opposition to Change

The most distinctive characteristic of a Fundamentalist is a blatant and overt opposition to change. Indeed, change disrupts the natural flow of the organization and represents a realignment of values. It is important to note that Fundamentalists enjoy practicing as professional educators. They enjoy the traditional aspects of the school as an institution. While observing and interviewing Fundamentalists, I saw a clear affinity for this tradition: Fundamentalists often speak fondly of the days when corporal punishment, curricular autonomy, and local control were part and parcel of our education system. They express a loathing for outside influence and control and administrators who dare to try and control operations in their classrooms. Where does this tendency to cling to the past come from?

A sociological study conducted by Dan Lortie (1975) revealed some critical information about teachers. Lortie was able to observe two very important variables that may explain the behavior of Fundamentalists:

1. Teachers have been socialized in the field where they have practiced since they were 5-year-old children and have not been removed from that context since entering kindergarten.

Since age 5, educators observed others' practice in the field in which they would eventually practice themselves. Lortie calls this phenomenon the "apprenticeship of observation."

2. On average, teachers were very good students and occupied the highest levels of the organization. As teachers, they bring that experience to the classroom and seek to preserve the same system that they enjoyed and benefited from as students.

Lortie concluded that it is irrational to expect people who benefited from a system to be the catalyst for changing that system. In fact, we should expect them to try and preserve a personally beneficial system. This helps explain why Fundamentalists would have such reverence for the norms and values of traditional school and why they would feel threatened if those traditional ideas were challenged or eventually replaced. The educator's own personal experience in school, according to Lortie, is the single most important variable in the current paradigm of the schoolteacher.

Lortie's research is helpful in clarifying many of the values that Fundamentalists hold dear; Fundamentalists collectively long for the way that schools used to operate. This longing can be described in what I call the *Old Contract* and the *New Contract.*

The Old Contract Versus the New Contract

The Old Contract represents the unwritten set of norms, values, and practices that defined the public school system for both students and educators before the advent of the accountability movement. The New Contract is the new set of values that promote transparency of school performance to the public, standardized curriculum and assessments, and proficiency ratings determined by nonmembers of the school community, along with the new educational strategies that support that system. In this case, the term *contract* refers to the universal set of expectations that guide every member of the school community and define their roles and responsibilities within the context of the public school system. In many cases, Fundamentalists entered the field while these long-held traditions were still in place, and they expressed discontent and anguish over the new paradigms and systems that have replaced them, which has further solidified their opposition to change in general.

The Old Contract provision that seems to find the most Fundamentalist approval is a teacher's right to autonomy. The most oft-repeated credo I heard from Fundamentalists was the teacher's right to control curriculum. From the very beginning of the evolution of American schools, teachers had the right to control what content they taught in their classroom. The Old Contract dictated that the system had the right to choose the general theme and focus for the class through some form of master course schedule (math, reading, algebra I, and so on), but the specific content to be covered during instruction was the exclusive right of the individual classroom teacher. The teacher determined the content of the lesson, how it was taught, and the pace of instruction.

The New Contract calls for a standardized curriculum. This curriculum is developed by a central body, usually a state department of education, and teachers are expected to teach students defined learning standards. Fundamentalists collectively display a dislike for "outsiders" such as administrators, boards of education, and politicians interfering with what many call their "creativity." A common complaint among those I observed was that they do not have enough time to be creative and teach what they want to teach to students because they have lost control of the curriculum. Fundamentalists are convinced that the standardized curriculum is detrimental to students, and they express this viewpoint to anyone willing to listen. They yearn to go back to the Old Contract, according to which teachers had the right to shut their doors and teach students the things they felt were most important to learn. The loss of the right to curricular autonomy has been particularly painful for Fundamentalists.

Fundamentalists also express displeasure with losing autonomy over evaluation. Under the Old Contract, teachers not only had the right to teach the things they felt students should learn, but they were afforded the right to be the sole assessors of student proficiency. Under the Old Contract, teacher judgment was the sole criterion for determining student academic success. Under the New Contract, proficiency is judged both internally and externally by student performance on standardized academic exams. Additionally, the New Contract has created an atmosphere that places blame on the teacher for failing to prepare students properly for success, whereas the Old Contract placed the blame on the student for not reaching proficiency. This represents a substantial shift in practice and philosophy.

The Old Contract recognized the teacher as not only the content expert, but also the instructional expert. The Old Contract assumed that teachers were not only knowledgeable about the subject they taught, by virtue of going through the rites of passage necessary to attain a professional teaching position, but also experts on how to teach that content. This assumption created space between the teacher and outside influences; teachers were the undisputed masters of their roles. The New Contract does not make such a defined distinction. The era of accountability has caused educators in leadership positions to become involved in instruction and instructional development in new ways. Stakes are high for school districts; if students do not excel on standardized tests, government officials want to know what school or district leaders plan to do to improve student performance. This new role of instructional leadership has particularly annoyed Fundamentalists. In my study, many Fundamentalists expressed displeasure with leadership activities such as administrative walk-throughs, common academic assessments, student achievement data, and other intrusions on instructional autonomy. They also resented the new push to constantly seek professional development and to use terms like *research based* and *best practice*. To Fundamentalists, these concepts and terms are an insult to their expertise and intelligence. They feel that the New Contract interferes with their ability to be as effective as they once were in their classrooms.

The Old Contract gave teachers freedom of interaction. If teachers chose to shut the door and avoid interaction with colleagues, they were free to do so. If their classroom was orderly, students behaved, and they attempted to teach their subject matter, teachers had the right to be left alone. In fact, when I started as a teacher more than 2 decades ago, my school culture taught me that I would be well respected among my peers if I could demonstrate that I could operate effectively without the help of others. So, under the Old Contract, not only did teachers have a right to work in isolation, they were *rewarded* for taking a position of isolation.

Under the New Contract, schools are demanding that teachers work together and collaborate as a new strategy to help student academic performance. Not only does the concept annoy Fundamentalists, but the terminology does as well. Fundamentalists do not feel the need to work with others. They feel that they have paid the price to enter the field and that they know enough to teach their students properly without attending collaborative meetings at the building or district levels. The overwhelming majority of the Fundamentalists I studied felt that meeting with other teachers was a waste of time and an intrusion of their right to control their working conditions. Having their day dictated and planned for them was not a part of the initial deal.

Finally, Fundamentalists hold resentment about the new role of students, parents, and the community at large. Under the Old Contract, students were admonished to obey and listen to their teachers or punitive measures would swiftly follow. At one juncture, teachers could physically punish students who did not comply. Under the Old Contract, it was the job of school leaders to support the teacher by either removing or punishing any student who did not comply with directives or posed a threat to classroom harmony. Fundamentalists were very comfortable with the principal's role under those circumstances. The Old Contract also dictated that parents had limited access and influence in the classroom. The teacher, and the school in general, prevailed in issues of grades, behavior, and privileges. The business of the school belonged to those who were the experts and professionals.

The New Contract looks very different. Litigious parents and a society with a thirst for negative media coverage have redefined how schools interact with the community. Administrators have to take into consideration school, district, and legal policies before disciplining a student. In fact, under No Child Left Behind, if a school fails to meet stated academic progress goals, the parent has the right to enroll their child in another school at the school system's cost (for transportation and so on). Fundamentalists feel that the New Contract has produced an anti-teacher climate in our schools.

It is very evident that Fundamentalists do not have much confidence or admiration for the current direction of public education. Fundamentalists do not view themselves as anti-education or anti-child;

they simply hold a different set of beliefs than those of the new era of public education. They feel that the Old Contract has a proven track record and is more fair and equitable than the New Contract.

Belief in the Normal Distribution

In chapter 2, we examined the phenomenon of the bell curve and normal distributions and established that in a normal distribution, equity is not the goal; rather, comparison and ranking are the goals. Herrnstein and Murray argued in *The Bell Curve* (1994) that this is simply the natural order of things, that all things are not equal and will never be equal; some human beings happen to be more talented, gifted, and capable than others, and anyone who does not acknowledge this reality is delusional. Fundamentalists hold a very similar paradigm.

As I interviewed Fundamentalist educators, I learned that they loathed accountability initiatives like NCLB, and they did not agree with the mantra that "all children can learn." One Fundamentalist told me that "it is impossible for every kid to excel in school. Some of them are cut out for school, and some just are not. I listen to the principal giving 'lip service' about believing in all kids, but he knows as well as I do that that just isn't going to happen." This statement was typical of a Fundamentalist response to the egalitarian ideal that schools can be places where equity in learning is possible.

Even more interesting, each Fundamentalist with whom I had an opportunity to interact did not feel that his or her stance was pessimistic or anti-child. They felt their viewpoint was simply more realistic—that anyone who believed every child in the United States could read and perform mathematics at grade level by the year 2013 was either not rooted in reality or under the influence of a controlled substance! In the mind of the Fundamentalist, educators and politicians who promote universal achievement for students need a paradigm shift. In fact, some Fundamentalists expressed that they believed egalitarian idealism is in fact damaging for kids who face tremendous obstacles to school performance like poverty and unfit parents. One Fundamentalist expressed concern that these students felt they were "set up for disappointment." She elaborated by saying, "These kids do not need to be fooled into believing they can all go to college when many of them were born crack-cocaine dependent or suffered from fetal alcohol syndrome." She felt that they would be better off if they instead had more access to trades or classes where they could "use their hands." One Fundamentalist supported this worldview with a simple statement: "We live in a world where some people are doctors, and some people pick up garbage." He and others felt that this societal polarization was the natural order of things, and who was he to mess with nature?

Fundamentalists can be accurately described as *social Darwinists.* Social Darwinism was described by sociologist Robert Bannister (2008) as:

> The idea that humans, like animals and plants, compete in a struggle for existence in which natural selection results in "survival of the fittest." Social Darwinists typically deny that they advocate a "law of the jungle." But most propose arguments that justify imbalances of power between individuals, races, and nations because they consider some people more fit to survive than others. (p. 1)

Social stratification is a norm to Fundamentalists. They believe that some people, for some reason, are simply more capable than others, and this natural and eternal imbalance is a function of the universe.

Upon examination of Fundamentalists' classroom performance, I discovered that their paradigm was not only philosophical—they also translated this belief system into practice. Their student grade distribution generally held to the standard of a normal distribution of performance. They assigned a small percentage of As, and the vast majority of students received Bs, Cs, and Ds, and usually a small proportion of students received Fs. This was true except in classes that were made up of large numbers of students labeled at risk or honors. In these cases, the grade distributions were skewed to either pole depending on the makeup of the class.

The Fundamentalists also shared similar discipline patterns. They did not write excessive amounts of referrals; they simply referred students for discipline who fit the typical profile of students in need of control through punitive methods. These students included a disproportionate amount of minority students and male students who did not excel at the secondary level. At the elementary level, they disproportionately referred students who did not display grade-appropriate maturity. In many cases, they also encouraged administrators to test students for placement in special education.

There was a clear disconnect between student performance and teacher responsibility among the Fundamentalists I observed. Fundamentalists clearly believed that students should sink or swim on their own merits. Those who excel deserve the fruits of their labor, they suggested, and those who do not excel deserve their fate because of a lack of personal commitment or ability. They expressed little to no empathy for students who were not successful, and they also did not try to take credit for the students who excelled. Their job was to allow nature to take its course.

Skill Levels

Like Believers, Fundamentalists display a wide range of professional skills. I observed some Fundamentalists who displayed very low levels of content knowledge and pedagogical skills and others who displayed high levels of knowledge and used very effective teaching strategies with their students.

A Fundamentalist is not an ineffective teacher by virtue of his or her political stance. But certain values Fundamentalists hold dear make it very difficult for them to promote a healthy school culture. Fundamentalists who I observed using very effective teaching strategies were effective with the students that they were entrusted to educate, but they still refused to work effectively with other professionals or embrace any form of change, and they had a generally negative disposition about the motives and ability of their leaders.

I contend that even the most effective Fundamentalists still pose a threat to a school's culture and its achievement of universal success for all students. Even though they show pockets of effectiveness and proficiency, they are not poised to embrace techniques and strategies that could allow them to be even more effective. Obviously, a Fundamentalist who does *not* exhibit effectiveness in the classroom is an even bigger problem. An ineffective professional who rejects change presents a danger to any organization.

Warring Paradigms

Of all of the members of the school community, Fundamentalists are by far the most active. They actively and consistently seek to add to their ranks and to gain political power to support their belief system. They are very active within the formal and informal organization, and their level of commitment to achieving their end is much more intense than that of the Believers. Watching them operate within several different school systems revealed a savvy, well-organized, and determined group of individuals.

Emotional Versus Rational

One characteristic of Fundamentalists that became evident during my observations was their commonly used strategy of keeping the philosophical argument focused on emotion. They regularly engaged in debates, sometimes arguments, with staff members with opposing viewpoints. During these debates, they centered their arguments about how a proposed policy change or change in practice affected them and other staff members on the emotional issues associated with the change—on comfort, convenience, and working conditions.

At an elementary school, I observed a school-improvement team meeting at which the Fundamentalists quickly took control. The meeting consisted of seven staff members from the school: five teachers, one school psychologist, and the principal. The topic of discussion was a proposed change in the recess schedule: under the new plan, students would receive a recess of 20 minutes daily, which was in compliance with state law and met the teacher contractual time allotment, instead of the 30 minutes they currently received. Recess at this school was traditionally supervised by lunchroom aides, and that would continue under the principal's proposed plan. Teachers typically used the 30 minutes per day to plan lessons, correct papers, or for other school-related work. The principal explained that the extra 10 minutes per day would be used to extend a literacy block for students and that this extra time was critical for struggling readers, especially in grades 3 through 5.

Her proposal met immediate resistance by two of the seven members who were Fundamentalists. As the first teacher responded, she spoke as if she had gathered a coalition of teachers who felt that they currently had too much responsibility, and taking 10 minutes from the 30 minutes of undirected teacher time would cause immediate resistance within the ranks of teachers. The second teacher expressed concern about infringements on her "personal time." She expressed concern about losing control of noninstructional time, and suggested that giving in to this proposal might be the beginning of a domino effect that could develop into a total loss of control of professional time, both instructional and noninstructional.

The principal appeared to be unprepared for their responses. She immediately tried to meet them at an emotional level by questioning their commitment to the fundamental purpose of the school. She expressed concern about what she considered "professionals squabbling over a mere 10 minutes per day." The principal missed the point. Her anger at the answers of the two Fundamentalists created a psychological impasse that caused both parties to retreat to their corners, and the issue remained unresolved. The other members of the team sat silently at a distance as the Fundamentalists went to battle with the school principal.

What lay at the heart of the position of the two Fundamentalists?

- Personal comfort

- Attachment to their daily routine

- Resistance to giving up power

The principal fell right into the emotional argument of the Fundamentalists, and they achieved exactly what they intended: *protection of the status quo*. Fundamentalists thrive at the emotional level. They rarely challenge an organizational change supported by research and empirical evidence concerning the purpose of schooling and effective education of children. What is even more fascinating is that Believers, both teachers and administrators, rarely challenge Fundamentalists with research-supported arguments.

The principal in the meeting I observed was offering changes that would support the stated goals of the organization. She wanted to improve the literacy skills of her students, especially at the upper elementary level where students performed more than 20% below the state average on her state's standardized reading test at grades 3, 4, and 5. She could have buttressed her case with research supporting longer exposure to effective literacy strategies to promote student proficiency in reading. Instead, she allowed the Fundamentalists to engage her in an emotional argument, the catalyst for yet another Fundamentalist victory in her school. Things remained the same, despite the fact that large numbers of students did not achieve at acceptable levels academically.

If Believers are to effect change, they must engage Fundamentalists in discussion. Believers should remember that engaging a Fundamentalist in an emotional battle is not a recipe for success. Believers must instead use the following strategies:

1. Clearly state the reason for the change proposal.

2. Connect the change proposal to the foundational purpose of the school and the stated improvement goals with the use of objective information (data).

3. Support the proposal with empirical and anecdotal evidence of effectiveness from several different sources.

This three-step approach erodes the Fundamentalists' argument at the foundation. It reasserts the fact that schools are built for the education of children. It puts students at the center of the argument, and it makes it difficult for Fundamentalists to publicly advocate for a stance that clearly hurts children. Finally, this type of approach forces Fundamentalists to present an equally compelling argument supported by empirical evidence. When Believers used these strategies in the schools I observed, the Fundamentalists' political power took a major hit, especially in formal organizational settings.

Formal Versus Informal Culture

Organizational theorists agree that every organization has both a formal and informal structure. This concept was first introduced by Henry Landsberger, who analyzed the famous study of the Hawthorne

Works Plant in Cicero, Illinois, from 1924–1932. The findings from this study sparked a series of important findings in workplace relations and employee productivity (Pyoria, 2007).

The *formal organization* consists of all the official arms of the organization. These branches of the organization have been officially sanctioned by the organizational structure. These branches consist of official committees, task forces, and teams such as school improvement teams, curriculum committees, and the Parent Teacher Association (PTA). Parts of the formal organization are monitored and evaluated against the organization's norms and goals.

The *informal organization* consists of all of the covert alliances that develop as a result of interaction in the formal organization. These alliances are not officially sanctioned, and their goals are created by their members, so they are only governed by those who participate. They have no formal rules. The goals of an informal alliance are generally not in alignment with those of the formal organization, which often makes the informal organization a threat to the productivity and longevity of the formal organization (Pyoria, 2007). Fundamentalists work very effectively in the informal organization.

It became very clear after spending hours observing and interviewing Tweeners that they were prime targets of Fundamentalist recruitment in informal organization. These informal situations tended to form in staff lounges, staff parking lots, during telephone or email conversations, at official and unofficial staff social events, and in the halls of the school. These informal places allowed the Fundamentalist to bond with other Fundamentalists and potential Fundamentalists. In these informal arenas, Fundamentalists can control the agenda and form the argument. Believers are intentionally omitted from informal Fundamentalist alliances unless they are viewed as potential converts.

Unless a school leader concerned about improving the quality of student learning is skilled in organizational politics, these informal alliances could easily go undetected and work against progress. A school leader must always be aware of the conversations happening around him or her, both formal and informal, and develop the skill of "erasing the line" between the informal and formal organizations. Staff members must become as comfortable expressing their views in the public forum, under the norms and values of the formal organization, as they are expressing them in the privacy of the informal organization. In order to accomplish this end, leaders must accomplish the following two objectives:

1. Create frequent opportunities for Fundamentalists to voice their viewpoints, and be prepared to refute potential arguments against change initiatives by stating a better and more profound public case.

2. Extend a public olive branch to opposing viewpoints by encouraging intellectual dialogue about organizational goals. This strategy will help others see that leaders are not seeking to perpetuate division among staff members, and they may come to view Fundamentalists' informal recruitment as unethical.

The Three Ds

The pattern of the Fundamentalist is very predictable. I observed Fundamentalists using three primary methods of influence to achieve their political ends: defamation, distraction, and disruption. These methods were sequential, and the intensity of their potency declined with the use of each method.

Defamation

Within the most stagnant and toxic of school cultures, Fundamentalists rule by intimidation. They are not shy about letting visitors know that they control the direction of the organization. At this very toxic stage, leaders must be extremely careful about the approach they take when initially challenging the Fundamentalists' control of the organization. The first method I observed Fundamentalists using when threatened was defamation—an all-out personal assault on the change agent. When someone challenges a toxic culture, Fundamentalists most often attack the individual advocating the change.

In my study, I witnessed this form of assault at a middle school situated in a suburban school district near a major Midwestern city. The district used to be very racially homogeneous (white) and middle class. During the previous 10 years, the district experienced a huge transformation of demographics both racially and economically. In 2006, the school district was 91% African American, and 40% of the students in the district were from homes that were economically disadvantaged.

The district was experiencing all of the typical transition issues associated with this type of massive cultural and economic change in the community. Juwanza Kunjufu (2002) identifies these struggles in the following manner:

- There is a cultural disconnection between the experienced staff and the new student population.

- School employees, particularly teachers and administrators, do not reflect the student body racially, culturally, and economically.

- There is a policy and systemic disconnection between the school system and the new members of the community.

The district hired its first African American superintendent in 2002, and one of her initial goals was to hire a more diverse staff with an emphasis on district and building leadership. This initiative did not bode well with the teacher and administrator union leaders, who claimed that past practice dictated that the district promote experienced teachers with long-term histories and commitments to the district to key positions of leadership. The unions felt that intentionally seeking candidates on the basis of race would damage that long-standing tradition of awarding leadership positions to those who knew the district best.

The superintendent did not agree with the union's assertion. She felt that leadership positions had been traditionally given to experienced teachers who were politically connected and who wished to pad their retirement packages by spending the final years of their educational careers as administrators who enjoyed higher salaries. The superintendent presented the board of education and the union with data from the past 20 years illustrating that the typical building principal was in the twilight of his or her career and stayed in the position an average of 3.2 years. She argued that not only did the district need more diverse representation in the ranks of leadership, but that the "good ol' boy" system of politically motivated leadership assignments needed to be changed as well.

The middle school hired an African American woman to serve as principal in 2005. She was not only the first African American principal, but also the first woman to serve in that position. Additionally, she was the first external hire for this leadership position in the previous 18 years. She had over 25 years of experience as a teacher and administrator in a large urban school district. The superintendent appointed her to the position based on her impressive interview with the superintendent and her cabinet. The building teaching staff was not involved in the interview process for the new principal, despite the fact that teachers had been involved in that process for over 30 years. It was well known that many staff members wanted to see the current assistant principal, a former teacher, promoted to the top position.

The fundamentalists were upset with these new developments for several reasons:

- The traditional system of promotion to leadership was dismantled. This new reality might affect some Fundamentalists directly and affect their future plans and incomes.

- The new superintendent disregarded the traditional power structure. The unions had been powerful forces in demanding the conditions for selecting personnel. If the unions lost political power, Fundamentalists' input and power as district employees was in jeopardy.

The new principal represented this great shift in control of power. Though the vast majority of the experienced teachers who embraced the traditional district system and policies were white, some were African American. In fact, about one-third of the staff was African American. Their issue with the new principal was motivated by power: They sought to maintain a system that they felt was more personally beneficial.

The Fundamentalist defamation campaign against the new principal had two facets. The first case they tried to make was that her experience in an urban district was not compatible with what they needed in their suburban district. Many of the Fundamentalists referred to her as the "ghetto principal" in private. The second case they tried to establish centered on her student disciplinary philosophy. The new principal wrote a memo to the staff in the first month of her tenure in response to what she considered to be a high number of disciplinary referrals for students. She believed that a student should only be suspended from school under the most extreme circumstances. The Fundamentalists ran with this philosophy and tried to make the case that student conduct was out of control and the school was going in the wrong direction.

The Fundamentalists were very active in the informal organization, making the case to both staff members and parents that the urban experience of the principal was subpar, and she was unprepared to lead a traditionally high-achieving school. Fundamentalists openly discussed what they considered her lack of qualifications with anyone who would listen. The defamation campaign about the student suspension issue was played out in several different courts. This issue made its way into the gossip circles, but there were also two formal employee grievances filed on behalf of staff members who felt that her leadership made the building "unsafe" for students and teachers, even though the facts revealed that under her tenure, serious student violations like assaults, drug use, weapon possession, and theft were down significantly from the previous school year.

This two-pronged approach caused such uproar within the school and community that the board put pressure on the superintendent to reassign the principal after just 2 years of service at the middle school. The union leaders used the ousted principal's "failure" as a rationale to reinstitute the old site-based interview process that they claimed was more effective. The superintendent did not want to honor this request, and at the time of the conclusion of my study, the issue still had not been resolved.

The new principal represented a threat to everything that the Fundamentalists had come to know and depend upon. They believed that if they allowed this administrative appointment to go unchallenged, nothing would be off limits. Their actions were motivated by the need for power and control, and defaming and undermining the new principal was just collateral damage.

This aggressive campaign of defamation is not unfamiliar to our culture. Modern political campaigns are rooted in the notion that if we publicly destroy and humiliate our opponent, we increase our chances of success (Chang, Park, & Shim, 1998). Our culture seems to have a fascination with scandal, and being caught in a scandal is extremely damaging. Fundamentalists choose defamation as a tool of organizational control because it is so effective.

Disruption

When defamation is not enough, Fundamentalists turn to disruption and delay the implementation of policies or strategies that will force them to change their practices. So if the messenger cannot be stopped, the change initiative itself becomes the target.

On several occasions, I observed Fundamentalists engaged in creating what I call *miscellaneous scenarios*: obstacles to implementation of change that are so overwhelming that the staff loses confidence in the proposed change. For example, an interdisciplinary middle school team met about a proposed change to their team's student homework policy. A team member I had identified as a Believer initiated the proposal. The rationale for the policy change was data given to the team by the district academic office; the data showed that during the first semester of the school year, 40% of their students had either a D or an F on their report cards. This number was much higher than the district average of just over 20%. The policy change proposed the following provisions:

- Students would be allowed to turn in assignments after the due date, with a penalty to be determined by the team.

- Students would have an amnesty period of 2 days during which they could voluntarily enter a homework-assistance hour to be held after school. Teachers would volunteer their time and rotate the duty of supervising this homework-assistance hour.

- Teachers would send a letter to students' homes to notify parents when students were missing two assignments, and teachers would make a personal phone call when students had more than four missing assignments.

These proposals triggered a barrage of "What if?" scenarios from the vocal Fundamentalist on the team. She immediately attacked not the philosophical or theoretical aspects of the proposal, but the logistical aspects. Before considering the provisions of the proposal, she made the following rebuttals:

- "What if students wait until the last possible moment to turn in their assignments, and we get stuck grading a lot of papers?"

- "Who is going to decide the varying degrees of 'late'? Will vacation and school missed due to weather be calculated in how we identify late assignments?"

- "What if a student turns in an assignment that was due in the previous grading period? Do we still change their grade?"

In no way am I proposing that a person who legitimately challenges the details of a change initiative is a Fundamentalist. In fact, critical consideration of exactly what change would be most effective for students is typical of a Believer who is concerned about organizational effectiveness. A person who questions the wisdom of a decision of a school leader is not necessarily exercising fundamentalism—he or she may have a very legitimate concern that deserves to be heard. The difference is that the Fundamentalists' objective through this line of questioning is not increasing or maintaining effectiveness, but obstructing change. It became very apparent to members of the team in the example that the Fundamentalist teacher was not concerned about legitimate answers to her questions. Her goal was to create as many obstacles as possible to block the actual implementation of this or any strategy that would alter her practice. As the teacher who proposed the initiative answered each question posed by the opposing teacher, it became clear that no answer was good enough to gain the Fundamentalist's compliance. The other two teachers on the team, both Tweeners, dared not challenge either the Believer or the Fundamentalist and stayed neutral.

The teachers reached a stalemate, the issue was eventually dropped, and no change in policy or practice was implemented.

In addition to this strategy of obstruction, Fundamentalists also try to make the case for avoiding change by identifying past ineffective attempts to solve a similar problem. Fundamentalists often try to represent coalitions that may or may not exist; they pretend as if they are the voice of many and thus have to step forward to speak for those who will not speak for themselves. Their message is this: "You may think you understand what the staff needs, but I know how the staff *really* feels." They might also share other schools' nightmare stories of attempts to implement similar initiatives. They try and paint a picture that says to the change agents, "This does not work, and everyone knows it except you."

Distraction

The last and least powerful method of resistance is distraction. When Fundamentalists realize that they cannot stop the change agent or the change initiative, they begin to display passive-aggressive behavior that articulates to the rest of the staff that they are being forced to change, and they do not agree or like it.

These behaviors include nonverbal communications such as eye-rolling, assuming a negative posture, and engaging in an unrelated activity (like grading papers) during the planning or implementing of change. They will also freely share negative comments. When all viable avenues to blocking change appear to be closed, Fundamentalists retreat into a covert form of personal resistance. This form of resistance has no observable effect except to annoy others in the organization as a form of protest. In the study, Fundamentalists exhibiting this behavior usually complied with organizational decisions for change, but they were not willing participants. Schools that seek a healthy school culture and embrace change as a strong part of that healthy culture can deal with Fundamentalists at this level. These strong school cultures articulate the fact that behavior is more important than disposition. "It is good if you intellectually and emotionally embrace the critical change," they say, "but it is more important that you practice the change."

A Necessary Evolution

Fundamentalists pose the biggest and most critical challenge to schools seeking to create a healthy school culture. Their political stance is rooted in their perception that change is the enemy, and they organize to protect their very narrow view of how schools should operate. Leaders in the public schools of the 21st century and beyond must realize that change is an inevitable part of organizational evolution. Those who are not poised to evolve and meet the ever-changing needs of the students they serve are doomed to eventually fail.

Education is too critical to our society for leaders to allow it to be hijacked by a group of individuals who refuse to embrace substantive change, even in the face of compelling evidence. Fundamentalists might not have malicious intent, but their actions threaten to stunt the growth of the schools that serve our most needy students. School leaders and the Believers in our public school system have to become more active and vocal and meet this challenge of overcoming fundamentalism head on. In the next two chapters, we will take a look at real solutions that may curtail or eliminate fundamentalism altogether if applied properly.

CHAPTER 7

"Drop Your Tools"
A Lesson in Change and Our Best Chance at Eliminating Fundamentalism

The primary problem in a toxic school culture is an inability to properly respond to challenges and adversity. Educators in such a culture become stagnant, and their stagnation can be the catalyst for regression. Fundamentalists' resistance to change maintains the status quo when schools should be ahead of the curve and actively seeking strategies that will allow them to fulfill their ultimate goal to the best of their ability: universal student achievement.

So in their attempt to evolve and develop a productive school culture without staff division, schools must consider two key questions:

1. What is the right change for us to embrace?

2. How do we get all of our staff members to embrace this change and actively apply the right methods once we have identified them?

In *Good to Great* (2001), Jim Collins calls the process of answering these questions "getting the right people on the bus." Stephen Covey (1989) describes this process as *synergy*, which is a combination of the words *synchronization* and *energy*. According to Covey, when all the members of an organization have their missions and purposes aligned and combine that alignment with energy, they create a powerful force.

If people who lead businesses and other organizations understand and embrace these concepts, why don't school employees embrace the same concepts and set the standard for organizational effectiveness?

No industry has more on the line than education. If we are going to produce better and more prepared students, school culture must become aligned in purpose and collective focus on student achievement. Anything less than a unified effort will continue the trend of falling short in our goal for students.

DuFour, DuFour, & Eaker (2008) sum up the challenge of aligning paradigms and operating under the synergy advocated by Covey:

> Contemporary educators are being called upon to fulfill a new purpose—high levels of learning for all students. . . . To meet that challenge, educators must do more than write catchy mission statements; they must align the structures and cultures of their institutions to support their new mission. They must act in new ways. (p. 115–116)

Taking into consideration the various political agendas of the four groups identified in this book, especially the Believers and Tweeners, how can school leaders accomplish this synchronization and solidarity of focus necessary to create powerful schools? To find this answer, I would like to use a concept I call *educational pathology*.

Pathology is the scientific study of the nature of disease and its causes, processes, development, and consequences. As an education concept, pathology demands that a change agent carefully study the origin of a particular problem first to gain a clear understanding of its development. Once a leader has traced the origin and identified the cause of the problem, the solutions necessary to solve the problem become clear. This strategy makes the leader look deeply into the root of the problem so that reactions will not be surface-level and solutions will not be short-lived. The leader will be able to clearly ascertain the conditions that caused the problem and the mentalities that may have contributed to it. This concept assumes that holistic examination and complete understanding of a problem will lead to focused and effective solutions.

We can use educational pathology in our quest to eliminate the effects of fundamentalism in our school culture by examining the very nature of organizational resistance. We must consider the following questions:

• Why do people resist change?

- What conditions motivate people to change?

- How can leaders create the conditions that would motivate people to accept change?

"Drop Your Tools"

There is no study more qualified to explain the conditions that prevent people from changing than the Drop Your Tools research (Weick, 1996). This research examines firefighters' reactions during two significant forest fires: Mann Gulch in western Montana and South Canyon in Glenwood Springs, Colorado. Both of these fires resulted in high numbers of firefighter casualties. Though the firefighters were given direct orders by their supervisors to "Drop your tools and run!" many firefighters chose not to run, even though there were clear opportunities to change course and save their own lives. In this study, Karl Weick posed two questions:

1. Why is change so complex?

2. Why would a person refuse to change at the risk of losing his or her own life?

Weick thought that if we could understand why a person would reject change in the face of grave danger and ignore the first law of nature—survival—then we could understand the root of all resistance to change. Weick's work in this area provides powerful insight into human resistance to change.

The first disaster, the fire at Mann Gulch, was made famous in Norman Maclean's book *Young Men and Fire* (1992). On August 5, 1949, 14 young smokejumpers, their foreman Wagner Dodge, and a forest ranger were trapped near the bottom of a slope in western Montana by an exploding fire. Thirteen of these men were killed when they tried to outrun the fire, ignoring two orders—one to drop their heavy tools and one to lie down in an area burned off by an escape fire. Dodge survived by lying down in the cooler area created by the escape fire, and two others lived by escaping through a break in the rocks at the top of the slope (Weick, 1996).

At South Canyon, outside Glenwood Springs, Colorado, a similar event occurred 45 years later on July 6, 1994. Again, it was late on a hot, dry, windy afternoon as flames lit the side of a gulch as firefighters moved onto steep slopes and into dense, highly flammable forest to fight the fire. A wall of flames quickly raced up the hill toward the fire-fighters. They could not outrun the flames, and 12 firefighters perished (Weick, 1996).

In both disasters, the firefighters who perished did not drop their tools or packs, which would have significantly increased their chances of escape. An analysis concluded that had they dropped their packs and tools, they could have moved more quickly while exerting the same amount of energy and "the firefighters would have reached the top of the ridge before the fire if they had perceived the threat from the start" (U.S. Forest Service, 1994, p. A3–5, cited in Weick, 1996).

Implications for Drop Your Tools

What possible lessons can we learn from these two tragic events? First and foremost, Weick points to the fact that they were both very prevent-able. The firefighters who perished did not have to die. Their resistance to guidance and their unwillingness to change their course, even when the evidence before them was overwhelming, reveals the ultimate case of fundamentalism. After examining the evidence at these two tragic events, Weick identified four key reasons why the firefighters did not drop their tools, and he rated the intensity of resistance from level one to level four based on the reason or rationale for resistance. His research provides key insight in the fight to get Fundamentalists to "drop their tools" and seek a more productive methodology. Fundamentalists in our schools also dis-play varied levels of resistance that are directly related to their reason or rationale for adopting the fundamentalist paradigm, so we will not only identify their reasons for resistance, but also rate their intensity from one to four, with one being the weakest and four being the strongest.

Level One Fundamentalists

People persist when they are given no clear reasons to change.

—Karl Weick

What makes a Level One Fundamentalist? They resist change because they were never provided with a clear rationale for change. They resist because they simply do not understand why they need to change. Weick illustrates this concept in his explanation of the trouble at Mann Gulch and South Canyon:

> At Mann Gulch, Foreman Dodge did little briefing of his crew throughout the incident. One of the few times he spoke to them was when he gave the order to drop their tools. When the accident investigation board asked Dodge to tell them what reason he gave for dropping tools (Dodge, 1949: 121), Dodge replied, "It wasn't necessary. You could see the fire pretty close and we had to increase our rate of travel some way or another." What was clear to Dodge may not have been as clear to the other 15, nine of whom were first-year smokejumpers and all of whom had more experience fighting fires in timber than in the dry grass where they now found themselves. At South Canyon, the firefighters who kept their tools were also not given a reason to drop them. No one told them that they were at the head of an onrushing fire, which is crucial information, because it was plausible for them to perceive that they were on the north flank of the fire. (p. 4)

The leaders of the fire crews at both Mann Gulch and South Canyon made critical mistakes at crucial times. They assumed that the firefighters saw things the same way they viewed them and understood facts and realities that they never formally explained. Simply because leaders understand the context and urgency of a situation does not mean that their followers share the same perspective. Information must be shared on a regular basis and clearly comprehended by the follower before compliance can be expected.

In a study of human cooperation, Terence Burham and Dominic Johnson provided some valuable insight on understanding Level One Fundamentalists. Burham and Johnson (2005) found that human beings resist cooperation when their cognitive need to understand is not fulfilled. This is human nature: the human psyche works against blind cooperation and seeks a logical explanation before charting an unfamiliar course. Therefore, the needs of Level One Fundamentalists are legitimate. They resist change, and will continue to resist change, until their need for a logical explanation is met. These findings provide great hope for influencing the behavior of Level One Fundamentalists and recruiting them to the ranks of Believers.

What do these findings tell us about administrative or leadership behavior? They teach us one critical lesson: *the absolute worst way to change human behavior is by creating an illogical mandate strictly on the basis of coercion.* An analysis of current educational policies would show us that this methodology has been used regularly and with very little effectiveness in the late 20th and early 21st centuries. No Child Left Behind, despite its noble goals, was introduced in this manner. Schools were told to improve student test scores immediately or face punishment. There was no logical case presented to the educators who had to implement this policy. It was introduced to the entire educational community as a blanket mandate. Educators were ordered to improve student performance without an explanation about why student performance needed to be improved. The methodology chosen to introduce the change created new Fundamentalists rather than reforming existing Fundamentalists. In fact, an entire sector of the education community came together to fight NCLB. Educators resisted the initiative because they were not provided with a clear reason to embrace this sweeping paradigm change.

Education leaders at the district and site level cannot repeat the mistakes of the federal and state governments. They cannot simply expect compliance from their subordinates because they can order them to make a change. School leaders must first make a clear and solid objective case for change before expecting people to embrace the change. Educators must appeal to the sense of service with which most educators enter the field as Tweeners. A solid objective case for change can be made by using some of the following information:

- Data and statistics that create a catalyst for change in an inspirational way, instead of in a threatening way

- Empirical research that paints a clear picture that a technique or strategy is more effective than the one currently practiced

- An organizational mission and vision that give a rationale for adapting a potentially more potent strategy

Level One Fundamentalists can be easily converted. The basis of their resistance is logical and easily fixed. Leaders must resist the urge to boss or coerce their way to change. Change is best and permanent when a meeting of the minds occurs and the change is intrinsic as opposed to extrinsic. When leaders start to clearly articulate rationale and fulfill their staff members' need to understand, they can quickly move these Fundamentalists to new levels of productivity in our school culture.

Level Two Fundamentalists

People persist when they don't trust the person who tells them to change.

—Karl Weick

Level Two Fundamentalists resist change because they do not trust the judgment or skills of the leader. They question the credibility of the leader, which in turns causes them to trust the credibility of the leader's guidance. Weick (1996) explains how this concept played out during the Mann Gulch and South Canyon fires:

> Members of the firecrew at Mann Gulch did not know Dodge well (U.S. Forest Service, 1949: 112), which made it hard for them to know how credible his orders and actions were. At South Canyon, the Prineville firefighters did not know the five smokejumpers mixed in with their crew, all five of whom had told the crew either to run or to deploy their shelters. These instructions were not legitimate orders, nor were they mentioned by trusted people. (p. 5)

Level Two Fundamentalists develop a general distrust of school leaders that may or may not have anything to do with current leaders. They tend to express their distrust in their leaders' motivations in the following ways. They think:

- School leaders are motivated by looking good and moving up the career ladder.

- School leaders are untrustworthy. They make promises to please others instead of providing honest feedback based on reality.

- School leaders are hungry for power and seek to dominate teachers.

- School leaders do not understand the plight of the modern teacher and are too far removed from the conditions of the classroom to be effective.

All of these issues develop out of an experience or series of experiences that caused the Level Two Fundamentalist to adopt this perspective. If school leaders hope to move Level Two Fundamentalists from fundamentalism to belief in the possibility of universal student achievement, they must bridge the trust gap. This trust gap has two key components: leader competence and character.

The leadership research is very clear when it comes to the correlation between effective leadership and trust. The U.S. Army identified what they refer to as the "23 Traits of Character" necessary for a person to effectively lead in the armed forces. There is no place where snap decisions and alignment between leader and subordinate are more important than on the field of battle, where every decision can mean the difference between life and death. Even under these extreme circumstances, leaders must be more than just knowledgeable; troops have to trust them before they will follow a leader's commands. The U.S. Army's 23 Traits of Character are listed in the feature box below (U.S. Department of Defense, 1973, p. 7–8).

The United States Army's 23 Traits of Character

1. Bearing	13. Will
2. Confidence	14. Assertiveness
3. Courage	15. Candor
4. Integrity	16. Sense of humor
5. Decisiveness	17. Competence
6. Justice	18. Commitment
7. Endurance	19. Creativity
8. Tact	20. Self-discipline
9. Initiative	21. Humility
10. Coolness	22. Flexibility
11. Maturity	23. Empathy/Compassion
12. Improvement	

The business community is also very clear on the effects the character of a leader has on the productivity of an organization. The 2007 *Walker Loyalty Report,* which reports on workplace loyalty, noted that trust, especially in leadership, is the single biggest factor in worker retention (Baldoni, 2007). The study went on to cite several ways managers can boost their trust level with their employees. The strategies included:

- Do not make promises that cannot be kept.

- Back your people when it counts.

- Take responsibility and be publicly self-reflective when times are tough.

What can a school leader do to develop trust as the bridge to organizational health? First, he or she must realize that the Level Two Fundamentalist has a legitimate and real need for trust. If trust has been breached through a series of experiences, the resistant teacher will not move from his or her position until that need has been met. School leaders must remember that, in many cases, the emotional gap that Level Two Fundamentalists display may not be a direct result of anything the leader has personally done; rather, it may be the result of a collection of bad experiences in the past that the current leader must fix. It may seem unfair, but the Level Two Fundamentalist's need still exists, and the school culture is held hostage until that need is met.

Trust is broken in the eyes of the Level Two Fundamentalist when he or she questions the character and competence of a leader. To bridge this gap, the leader may consider the following strategies:

- Hold regular and public celebrations for the accomplishments of both teachers and students.

- Stay away from the limelight, and exhibit true humility.

- Do not violate rules you expect others to follow and for which you hold them accountable.

- Frequently use the pronoun *we* when publicly discussing the accomplishments or future plans of the school.

- Make good on your word. Do what you promise you will do.

- Do not ostracize Fundamentalists for holding different opinions. Guarantee them their right to their opinion in a way that preserves their dignity, even if you philosophically disagree with them.

In the area of competence and trust, school leaders may bridge the gap in the following ways:

- Know your stuff! Stay well versed in the evolving knowledge base of education.

- Lead teachers in the process of learning. Expose them to knowledge that enlightens their practice and gives them a new context.

- Familiarize yourself with the history of the school and community, and articulate a vision that will inspire others to think in new ways.

- Continue to improve your skills and credentials. Nothing says competence like a person who exhibits the quality of lifelong learning.

Level Three Fundamentalists

People may keep their familiar tools in a frightening situation because an unfamiliar alternative . . . is even more frightening.

—Karl Weick

Level Three Fundamentalists are educators who resist change because they are unsure if the change will cause them more stress, and perhaps still not achieve a better result than their current methodology. Weick (1996) shared the following analysis of the events at Mann Gulch:

People at Mann Gulch found it hard to drop their tools, but they found it even harder to comprehend the function of Dodge's escape fire. No one followed Dodge in, and some thought the fire was supposed to serve as a buffer between them and the oncoming blowup (Sallee, 1949: p. 77). It is equally strange to be told to deploy a fire shelter. Firefighters do not get much practice deploying fire shelters. Furthermore, it is tough to open a shelter while running in turbulent winds, with gloves on, and while looking for a clear flat area in which to lie down. (p. 5)

In stressful situations people make tough choices, and the firefighters were no different. They had to decide between using methodologies that were familiar to them, even though the odds did not appear to be greatly stacked against them, or try a strategy that was new, complicated, and untested. This dilemma is familiar to teachers. To effectively move Level Three Fundamentalists into cooperation with Believers, leaders have to address two issues: proper preparation and incremental implementation of change.

People are more likely to embrace change when they are properly prepared for change. Many public schools are in a situation similar to the one the firefighters found themselves in at Mann Gulch. Many educators are bombarded with various change initiatives that neither make sense nor strike a particular chord. They are being asked to consider many possible alternatives while managing a sundry of responsibilities that occupy the vast majority of their time. Investing time, a rare and precious commodity for educational professionals, on all of the various reform initiatives that come across the principal's desk can have a numbing effect on educators. The constant need to put out fires and deal with issues that Stephen Covey (1989) calls *Quadrant 1 issues*—issues that are "urgent and important"—leaves little time to seriously consider the adoption of *Quadrant 2 issues*—issues that are "important but not urgent" (p. 37). According to Covey, growth is gained in Quadrant 2. When important issues are properly researched, pondered, and developed—without the anxiety and stress of urgent time-consuming factors—the quality of the developed ideas are much better than the ideas or decisions made in Quadrant 1. Quadrant 2 decisions impact overall operations in a profound way, and perhaps reduce the number of Quadrant 1 issues. Simply put, when people get a chance to think before they act, their decisions are much more sound.

School days are filled with important and urgent issues. Effective administrators will make progress with Level Three Fundamentalists when they make time for personal and professional growth for all teachers. The firefighters at Mann Gulch had a very limited perspective on change. The commands given by the chief were unfamiliar and ill-placed. Expecting people with very little professional development and growth opportunities to make critical decisions on important issues while simply trying to survive is not a good way to encourage change. In fact, many of the Fundamentalists I interviewed mentioned their frustrations with all of the varied change initiatives that they were forced to adopt. They complained of little to no training and no consideration from administration for all of the daily duties that were still their responsibility.

For a Level Three Fundamentalist, developing capacity and skill in an environment that is conducive to cognition will make adaptation to meaningful change much more likely when potentially powerful opportunities for growth are presented. Richard and Rebecca DuFour (2006) describe professional learning communities (PLCs)—environments conducive to cognition that make meaningful change possible. They note that "PLCs operate under the assumption that the key to improved learning for students is continuous job-embedded learning for educators" (p. 2). The DuFours describe the growth of educators as the catalyst for the growth of their students. This growth has to be job-embedded, which supports the idea of Quadrant 2 development advocated by Covey (1989).

While serving as principal at Levey Middle School in Southfield, Michigan, I led my staff in what became known as the *Learning Center Concept* (Buffum et al., 2008). The Learning Center Concept was an ongoing system of growth and development on a daily basis in critical areas of need for our teachers. This system poised my staff for change through intentional exposure to new ideas that would provide the cognitive framework for accepting the right change at the right time. The Learning Center Concept had the following characteristics:

- **Driven by data**—A team of educators examined our critical data to determine important areas of need. This also helped provide a rationale for change for our Level One Fundamentalists.

- **A foundation of relevant research**—The team of educators found relevant literature and research that supported growth in critical areas of need. Teachers were provided this information in advance and invited to participate in intellectual discourse.

- **Context**—Leaders were concerned about the teaching staff's tremendous daily workload, so they employed the concept of "addition by subtracting" by eliminating traditional staff meetings and instead dedicating that time to professional growth. No new time requirements were added to the teachers' load to facilitate a proposed activity.

- **Collaboration**—Teachers were placed in very diverse teams of study partners in which they could problem solve and share insights.

The opportunity to interact with various schools of thought in a nonthreatening way on an ongoing basis opened many teachers up to the possibility of change who otherwise would have been closed to the idea. The environment and frequency of the Learning Centers eased their anxiety and prepared them for future school experiments that would make a real and transformational difference for their students. The engagement was gradual and ongoing so teachers did not feel they had to change course all at once. Improvement was focused on the long haul as opposed to short bursts of desperation.

Level Four Fundamentalists

People may refuse to change because change may mean admitting failure.

—Karl Weick

The last reason the firefighters refused to drop their tools gives insight to just how complex change can be for Level Four Fundamentalists. Weick describes this reason for resistance at Mann Gulch and South Canyon (1996):

To drop one's tools may be to admit failure. To retain one's tools is to postpone this admission and to feel that one is still in it and still winning. . . . Finally, implicit in the idea that people can drop their tools is the assumption that tools and people are distinct, separable, and dissimilar. But fires are not fought with bodies and bare hands, they are fought with tools that are often distinctive trademarks of firefighters and central to their identity. Firefighting tools define the firefighter's group membership, they are the firefighter's reason for being deployed in the first place, they create capability, they are given the same care that the firefighters themselves get (e.g., tools are collected and sharpened after every shift), and they are meaningful artifacts that define the culture. (p. 6)

Weick's argument is that some of the firefighters never planned to retreat, regardless of their circumstance. To run from a fire would be to redefine their purpose as firefighters. Firefighters are defined by their bravery and the willingness to run into the teeth of danger and save others. Running, and even more importantly, dropping the tools that were the symbols of their ability to save would undermine their own self-concept, therefore identifying them as failures. These firefighters would not have followed the commanders' request to retreat under any circumstances. According to Weick, the only way that the firefighters would have dropped their tools and retreated is if they were physically dragged out of the fire. Under no conceivable circumstance would they have chosen this option on their own.

Level Four Fundamentalists pose a particularly puzzling problem. There is not a lot that leaders can do to change their paradigm because they have defined themselves within the organization by their resistance to change. To drop their tools and cooperate, they would have to redefine themselves to the other members of the organization. Level Four Fundamentalists are so deeply rooted in their opposition to change that it consumes and defines them. They have no real observable needs except to be defined by their political position within the school.

There is only one real solution for Level Four Fundamentalists: strict monitoring. Leaders must send the message that the standards have changed, and the only way someone will be allowed to be comfortable is through compliance with the new school paradigm.

The skillful school leader should be able to effectively employ the strategies outlined in this chapter to significantly transform the paradigms of the Level One, Level Two, and Level Three Fundamentalists. Once the transformation takes shape at these levels, leaders should be able to isolate the Level Four Fundamentalists and use monitoring and coercion to force a change in behavior or a change in scenery. The illogical resistance of Level Four Fundamentalists will eventually call leaders into a battle of will. This is a fight that the school leader must win, because to allow Level Four Fundamentalists to operate in a school culture in the midst of effective transformation is akin to sanctioning the behavior. School leaders who understand that their true purpose is to lead an organization dedicated to service on behalf of students will not blink when this showdown arrives.

The monitoring tools available to leaders vary from place to place, but every school leader has some formal system to closely monitor unproductive and uncooperative employees. These tools generally include a trail of documentation of a teacher's performance with the intention of providing assistance for improvement with an ultimate consequence of termination of employment if performance does not improve. In many unionized states, this process is bargained, so the school leader must be careful to follow the mandated system of monitoring explicitly outlined in the master agreement. I have seen many administrators start down this road of formal monitoring of uncooperative teachers only to have the process interrupted or eliminated because of a loophole or a policy that was not followed properly. Where these agreements exist, school leaders must be very careful to make sure that the requirements of the master agreement have been satisfied. In areas where these agreements do not exist, leaders must be careful to make sure that whatever the district considers to be "due process" is honored and followed. The best case is that the mere presence of a formal system of monitoring creates a level of discomfort and anxiety in a Fundamentalist which will cause the Fundamentalist to focus on his or her own behavior.

School leaders often have the right of teaching assignment; they have the power to determine who teaches what and to whom. In many of the cases observed in this study, Fundamentalists sought and often occupied coveted teaching positions in schools, like teaching honors classes, while many Believers and Tweeners were assigned to much more challenging positions. Most significantly, leaders must place Level Four Fundamentalists in positions in the school where they are likely to do the least amount of harm to children. Second, assigning them to coveted positions sends the message to the rest of the staff that the behavior of the Level Four Fundamentalists is acceptable. In one of the middle schools involved in this study, a principal removed a Fundamentalist from his position as the social studies department chairperson and assigned him to a generic study skills class. The Fundamentalist was replaced in his chairmanship with a Believer, and the drastic change in working conditions caused him to quit and seek a position elsewhere. This may seem somewhat cruel or coercive, but the principal articulated to me that disappointing his former teacher was much more acceptable than disappointing his students, parents, and progressive staff members.

Ending Division

The good news is that Fundamentalists can be reformed and redirected in most cases. Level One Fundamentalists simply seek clarity in matters that involve changing long-held practices. School leaders can accommodate their requests very easily. Level Two Fundamentalists have an emotional need. Their experiences have created a general distrust of school leadership. A combination of exhibiting trustworthiness, ethics, humility, maturity, and patience can heal the very real wounds that Level Two Fundamentalists have and change their behavior for the better. Level Three Fundamentalists are uninformed, stretched, and overwhelmed. When leaders regularly address their knowledge gap, they provide a framework for not only understanding change, but eventually embracing it. Level Three Fundamentalists also need to see the long-range picture, and steady change spread over time works best for them as they struggle to deal with the myriad of responsibilities that hit them on a daily basis. Level Four Fundamentalists reject change because it potentially can redefine them and identify them as failures. Their goals are more important to them than those of the school, so leaders must use the tools at their disposal to hold them responsible for meeting new organizational standards.

This idea of producing synergy or getting the right people on the bus is not an easy one, especially for schools. Schools have limitations that businesses and other organizations do not have. Schools cannot simply terminate people who do not cooperate with their goals and replace them with more suitable professionals. Legal and employment regulations do not allow that. Creating healthy cultures in schools is a difficult endeavor, but it can and must be done. My hope is that this new framework can raise the likelihood that we can effectively win this battle and create the kind of school cultures that embrace and nurture our young people.

CHAPTER 8

Implications for Practice

When analyzing organizations, especially schools, it becomes clear that meaningful and productive growth is primarily a function of the cohesion of human resources. Technical or structural changes can certainly aid this process, but if the human factors are not healthy, growth and transformation become very difficult. This book has made a case for understanding why schools have such a difficult time changing when members of the culture cannot accept new paradigms that do not mesh with the traditional operation of schools.

Unfortunately, many school leaders find themselves underprepared to deal with all of the diverse aspects of school leadership, especially as it pertains to developing a healthy school culture (DuFour, 2001). This chapter will focus on practical methods that both administrators and teachers can use to loosen the grip of their Fundamentalists, overcome staff division, and focus the school on its primary purpose: student learning.

The schools I studied that were able to create and maintain a healthy school culture had some similar traits. They were all able to eliminate human distractions and call their colleagues to a higher, more professional purpose. This chapter will focus on three areas for action within schools and school systems:

1. Developing a systematic and schoolwide focus on learning

2. Celebrating the success of all stakeholders

3. Creating systems of support for Tweeners

A Systematic and Schoolwide Focus on Learning

Richard DuFour (2002) characterizes most ineffective schools as disorganized and unfocused institutions without a set of clear and focused goals. The schools I observed with the most toxic cultures demonstrated that assertion. A 1989 Northwest Regional Educational Lab report identified the most observable and effective leadership strategy in effective schools with healthy cultures. In these schools, leaders "framed school purpose policies in terms of one or two universal academic goals, which can in turn provide the framework for all other school activity" (Cotton, 1989, p. 71). This report also identified the turning point for transforming school culture: the change process begins with the tone of the relationship between the leader and teachers, which then trickles down to affect the relationship between teachers and students. In order to influence student learning at the classroom level, the school leader must begin by demanding that the organization as whole focus on student learning.

DuFour, DuFour, and Eaker (2008) assert that the first big idea of a professional learning community is a focus on learning. They explain that highly effective schools accept student learning as the fundamental purpose for their school. Leaders who are highly effective are skilled at focusing the entire organization on this purpose. DuFour, DuFour, and Eaker also point out that PLCs not only focus on effective classroom methods for improving student learning, but also consider the learning of all members of the school as the catalyst for improving student learning. DuFour and Eaker (1998) note that the first characteristic of a PLC is developing what they call shared mission, vision, values, and goals. They explain this process in the following manner:

> The mission question challenges members of a group to reflect on the fundamental purpose of the organization, the very reason for its existence. The question asks, "Why do we exist?" "What are we here to do together?" and "What is the business of our business?" (p. 58)

Schools that want to produce a healthy learning environment must first and foremost be clear about their collective purpose. As I observed in many schools, progress becomes nearly impossible if a collective commitment to service for the purpose for universal student achievement does not exist. The following section will provide some practical strategies for developing this collective sense of purpose.

A Collective Focus on Purpose

During my study, I observed school staffs that were united in purpose. Some of these schools had long ago developed their positive and productive cultures, and some were in the beginning stages of development. They all shared some common traits:

- Staff members used a common vocabulary when articulating matters of student expectations and classroom methods.
- Staff members engaged in problem-solving conversations and universally shunned complaints.
- Staff members exhibited a high level of efficacy where the school mission and purpose were concerned.

I recall one particular faculty meeting that was specifically focused on the fundamental purpose of the school. The principal was concerned that the school mission and vision statements were simply dogma and had no effect on the practices within her school. She led an activity with her staff that spanned three staff meetings and ended with a clear and universally accepted direction and mantra for their school.

As an experienced practitioner, I was not surprised that many of the staff members—especially the experienced ones—were not excited. This type of activity was not uncommon to many of them. Some revealed that on several occasions with past school administrators they had revamped the mission statement, but that such work proved to be an exercise in futility. Many complained that the exercises of the past were purely symbolic and had no real effect on day-to-day practices. They articulated three major problems with the mission debates of the past:

1. The prior attempts were unorganized. Staff members were simply asked, "What do you think our mission statement should say?"

2. People with strong opinions quickly dominated conversations. Anyone who challenged their opinions had to engage in an unproductive argument, which made the activity more divisive than cohesive.

3. No substantial changes occurred after weeks of painstaking arguments.

But it soon became clear that this meeting was unlike any other that the staff members had experienced in the past.

This principal's series of exercises was different for several reasons. First, the principal clearly stated the purpose of the activities up front: "We want to get on the same page so that we can make sure that our students are successful." She clearly articulated the research on cohesive school staffs and their effect on student achievement. This step may seem simple, but the problems that arise from lack of articulation of goals between leadership and subordinates are well documented. Organizations that move cohesively have established solid lines of communication that allow them to be more flexible and responsive to the needs of the organization (Wynn, 2006). Educators who become accustomed to the negative impact of "Do as I say" dictatorial leadership that has dominated schools of the past seem to embrace this type of transparent, collaborative leadership.

The second step in her process was to provide an accurate profile of the school's current performance as well as both educational and demographic data on the correlation between school performance and future life success. She created a compelling case for looking at alternative methods by demonstrating the failure of past paradigms and practices. Laying out the indisputable case for improving student performance put a human spin on the process. She was able to take the focus off of the teachers and their personal and individual needs and create an atmosphere that allowed them to collectively focus on what was best for the students.

After providing a compelling case for change, the principal divided the staff into discussion groups. Each group was armed with a comprehensive set of both achievement and demographic data on the students and community they served. She asked the discussion groups to consider the following questions:

1. Who are our students?
2. What strengths do they bring to the school?
3. What needs do they bring to the school?
4. How can we collectively enhance their lives?

Before releasing the groups for their collaborative discussions, she established a very clever set of group norms. She instructed the groups to eliminate the following phrases from their discussions about school direction:

- "I think . . ."
- "I feel . . ."
- "I believe . . ."

Her rationale was that a decision as important as re-establishing the very purpose of the school should not be subjective. If staff members were going to advocate for a particular focus or direction for the school, they needed to make an objective case by providing comprehensive data. These very clever additions to this process totally transformed the direction of the conversation when compared to similar activities conducted in the past. The principal and her assistant principal informally monitored the group discussions to ensure that groups followed guidelines of the activity, but offered very little input into the discussions.

This activity produced dialogue in ways that this school had never experienced before. Not only was the staff able to develop a cohesive and concise mission statement for their school, their dialogue prompted them to develop a 3-year plan of action focused on real change strategies that embodied their public statement of purpose. This renewed and uniform focus on purpose developed new energy among staff members. The language the staff used was noticeably different. The principal changed school policies and procedures that were not in alignment with their new mission. The staff also decided to sponsor a Parent Night where they articulated their new mission statement and plans for the next 3 years and asked parents to be partners in this process.

The principal at this school sought to define the purpose of her school around student academic achievement, and she was successful. She involved her entire staff, and staff members clearly took ownership in the process and voluntarily did things that coercion or manipulation could never accomplish.

Effect on School Culture

The focus of this school's mission activity was apparent: focusing all stakeholders in the organization on student achievement. The principal accomplished this end, but how did this affect the culture?

This activity, along with similarly structured activities, provided a strong catalyst for change for Level One Fundamentalists. These Fundamentalists resist change simply because they do not understand the rationale. This activity started with a complete and compelling presentation on the real effects of education in a student's life. Children who do well in school overwhelmingly succeed while those who do not complete school (or struggle in school) overwhelmingly lead painful and unproductive lives. The principal appealed to the heart of her educators. Her introductory activity sent this message: "If you were inspired to join the field of education to change the world, it is not going to happen under our current system." For a Level One Fundamentalist, rationale means everything. When they understand, they cooperate.

This approach also gives Believers a platform to articulate their belief systems. One of the only problems with Believers is that they do not challenge Fundamentalists nearly enough to make a difference. In fairness to the Believers, in most schools they are not given a platform to challenge those belief systems on a regular basis. Fundamentalists work well within the informal organization, and Believers may find that conversations in the teacher's lounge or during lunch are not the best places to wage an intellectual debate with Fundamentalists. Structured meetings and activities provide Believers with solid data and empirical evidence to back their belief system, and formal rules keep conversations focused on the stated objectives. In the meetings I observed, a structured format made it very difficult for Fundamentalists to seize control over the collaborative discussions.

In addition, this activity gave Tweeners an opportunity to regularly reconnect with the very reason they chose the profession: to help kids. With all of the various new and stressful activities thrust upon Tweeners, they can be easily overwhelmed and lose focus and purpose. Tweeners also enjoy hearing about and benefit from the expertise and experience of their colleagues. In the meetings I observed, Tweeners felt like they were a real part of the team, and the group activities served to humanize their colleagues with whom they did not have many opportunities to interact otherwise. The Tweeners found this process to be invigorating; it reinforced their rationale for choosing their career path. Simplifying and unifying the school purpose made the transition to the profession more palatable for new educators. It did not take away the stress of adjustment to all of the varied and complex tasks involved in their jobs, but it made the challenges seem more worthwhile.

Celebrating the Success of All Stakeholders

Celebration of success has long been debated in the leadership arena. Many traditional thinkers believe that workers are paid to do their jobs, so therefore they should execute their responsibilities without fanfare. They think meeting job-related goals is just a part of the job, and celebrating expected achievement is unnecessary and even counterproductive. On the other hand, an emerging body of literature asserts that human behavior is complex, and celebration or appreciation for prowess on the job is one of the best and smartest ways to improve worker productivity (Glanz, 2000). Studies have indicated that things like salary and opportunities to advance are very low motivators, but recognition of achievement and celebration of goal-attainment are much more powerful methods for increased productivity (Nelson, 2007). This new school of thought does not view celebratory strategies as unnecessary fluff; rather, it considers celebration essential to human performance.

Celebration in school provides consistent reinforcement about what is important. People often celebrate what they value, such as holidays and birthdays, for example. How schools celebrate learning and those who help students learn says a lot about how much the school values learning. Bolman and Deal (1995) describe organizational celebration in this way:

Ritual and ceremony help us experience the unseen webs of significance that tie a community together. There may be grand ceremonies for special occasions, but organizations also need simple rituals that infuse meaning and purpose into daily routine. Without ritual and ceremony, transitions become incomplete, a clutter of comings and goings. Life becomes an endless set of Wednesdays. (p. 82)

The positive school cultures I observed consistently celebrated the things the school valued. These celebrations were both planned and impromptu, and all were authentic. Recognition was genuine and not manufactured for the sake of giving the appearance of false appreciation in the midst of low productivity. These schools set clear expectations for all stakeholders—students, teachers, administrators, support staff, and parents. When these expectations were met, the achievements were celebrated proudly and publicly.

Institutionalized Celebration

One of the elementary schools I observed in my study found a very authentic and inexpensive way to consistently celebrate the attainment of their school goals. This school held staff meetings after school twice monthly, and awards were given at each meeting.

The school gave out *mobile awards*—trophies symbolizing prowess in one of four areas: leadership, curriculum, child advocacy, and creativity. The awards were originally distributed by the principal, and the recipients could keep and display their awards for 2 weeks. At the next staff meeting, the winners passed the honor on to a fellow staff member whom they observed exhibiting the quality that the award recognized.

Each staff meeting ended with the passing of the award from one staff member to another. The presentations were sometimes dramatic and sometimes emotional, but they were always authentic. The principal at the school had found a way for staff members to show genuine appreciation for one another in a public way that reinforced the goals of the school and produced a spirit of teamwork necessary to build a high-performing school.

The other benefits of this activity are more subtle, but even more powerful. By giving staff members a forum to speak positively about their colleagues, the principal was subtly changing a norm. Fundamentalists thrive in a culture of slander and defamation. If they can keep colleagues and leaders at bay by creating a culture of personal mistrust, their maintenance of the status quo has a fertile environment to prosper. When people start to trust one another and focus on service to students, they become more willing to accept change. In fact, they begin to embrace change for the benefit of their students and are more willing to take risks both pedagogically and organizationally. It is hard for Fundamentalists to stir up feelings of contempt and distrust when their colleagues show such genuine appreciation for one another on a regular basis.

The other subtle benefit was changing the focus in the school from looking for the negative to looking for the positive. Human beings are creatures of habit; once we develop a habit, it is hard to break. Members of toxic cultures develop habits that breed consistent fighting and contempt. Members of a healthy culture consistently look for ways to validate their efforts. By turning over the responsibility of recognition of achievement to the staff, the principal forced them to look for positive attributes of their colleagues instead of looking for the negative. If a staff member received a leadership award, he or she had to spend the next 2 weeks looking for the best example of leadership among the other staff members. Repeating this activity over the long term caused a real transformation in culture. Looking for the positive was now the norm.

Impromptu Celebration

Not all of the celebrations were planned and institutionalized. I observed several impromptu celebration strategies that sent messages that were equally clear. Many of these celebrations were recognitions of student achievement as well as staff accomplishments.

In one high school, students received a variety of recognitions for accomplishments that ranged from improving test scores to being prompt to a particular class for an entire week. This high school developed what they called the *Goodie Jar*. A large jar was placed in the staff lounge and filled with items gathered by the school secretary and counseling staff. Many of the goodies were donated by the community and business people as well as by the school store, athletic department, and the principal. Some examples of goodies include the following:

- Professional sporting tickets (donated by professional sports teams)

- Passes to school events (both athletic and social)

- Certificates for free items (donated by local business)

- Student privilege opportunities (free student parking passes, for example)

The items could be given to either students or fellow staff members, and the distribution was totally left to the staff's discretion.

The school secretaries, who organized and maintained this effort, had one rule: the jar must be empty by the end of each week. If they noticed by midweek that the jar was still full or nearly full, they sounded a collective alarm. They sent a barrage of emails, memos, and verbal notifications that more recognition had to take place. One secretary told me, "We have great kids, and they do great things every day, and they will not continue to show us their great side if we do not show how much we appreciate them on a regular basis."

Celebration and Positive School Culture

The schools that celebrated authentically on a regular basis created a great atmosphere for collegiality. Collegiality is not collaboration, but having colleagues who genuinely like and respect one another creates an atmosphere ripe for collaboration.

Consistent celebration provided the Believers with a comfortable school atmosphere. They felt at ease and more connected with the other members of the school because they felt as if their paradigm was the prevailing one. Many of the Believers in the study who worked in healthy school cultures consistently mentioned the many celebratory aspects of their school, and how recognition of proficiency and effort made them feel at ease and produced a sense of family.

Tweeners also benefited from the celebrations. Much of the recognition went to students and skilled veteran colleagues, but this did not seem to bother the Tweeners. The celebration of success inside and outside of the classroom helped the Tweeners see what the future held for them. It helped them realize that the current struggles that many of them faced were not permanent and that education is not a collection of depressed and disgruntled professionals. Many Tweeners mentioned the joy they felt seeing their students recognized on a regular basis, and they could identify their colleagues as professional role models because of the public recognition they received.

Fundamentalists seemed to benefit from celebration as well—especially Level Two Fundamentalists. The catalyst for Level Two Fundamentalists' resistance is a void in their trust of leaders. The leaders who celebrated regularly and authentically started the process of reshaping Level Two Fundamentalists' view of the role of leadership in the school. Because celebrations were authentic and all-inclusive, the leaders were indirectly building trust with more skeptical staff members. Fundamentalists are pessimistic about the likelihood of ever serving under an ethical and selfless leader, so leaders' willingness to honor others in selfless celebrations projects an image of high moral character that Fundamentalists yearn to see.

A System of Support for Tweeners

Effective school leaders, especially those managing high numbers of new teachers, must work very hard to properly develop and retain their Tweeners. Focusing attention on those with potentially influential contributions paid off for some of the effective school leaders I observed. These school leaders made a conscious decision to put the majority of their energy into properly grooming their new teachers as the catalyst for turning their toxic school culture into a healthy one over time.

A report by the National Education Association (NEA) identifies new teacher mentor programs as one of the most vital aspects of building and sustaining powerful public schools (Moire, 2008). The report points out that the most effective new teacher mentoring programs have several facets. Simply assigning one mentor and assuming that the one mentor can meet the diverse needs of the new teacher is probably not the most effective method. Rather, schools that are comprehensive and thorough and involve several members of the school community in the mentoring process are most effective at retaining and guiding new teachers.

In addition to not having the support of the entire school community, new teachers often feel the isolation of the classroom. No other professional faces this unique isolation. For most of their professional lives, teachers will be the only adult in their immediate area of practice. This can be hard for veterans, and it can be fatal for new teachers. One new California teacher stated that "beyond problem solving and professional development, new teachers' experiences can be enhanced simply by being connected to a friend" (Christensen, 2008, p. 1). This teacher felt the impact of daily professional isolation and created an online community for new educators as a virtual support system for one another. I observed several effective leadership strategies during this study that controlled for the isolation factor and connected new teachers to support systems in innovative and effective ways.

Finally, effective school leaders developed systems that intensely developed the skill level of their new teachers in ways that limited their struggles in the classroom and in the school in general. These leaders felt that if they could shorten the learning curve for their new teachers and help them experience success in the classroom, these teachers would be less likely to suffer from many of the hardships that most new teachers experience. They achieved this goal in two different ways: first, they made it acceptable to struggle and to seek help. In many of the toxic cultures observed, it was unacceptable to struggle. Struggle was a sign of incompetence, and the incompetent teacher drew the scorn of his or her supervisor. Consequently, these schools maintained a very high rate of teacher turnover. The effective schools publicized the fact that all professionals struggle, and they encouraged new teachers to articulate their struggles so that the school system could have firsthand information in order to assist new teachers with their transitions.

Second, effective school leaders developed meaningful and adequate professional development for new teachers focused on the areas in which new teachers struggle most. A program set up in Baltimore, Maryland, focused on the real and critical needs of new teachers. The program serviced 400 new teachers participating in the Baltimore Public School's New Teacher Training Institute, a voluntary 4-week summer program for newly hired teachers. Now in its 2nd year, the institute provides hands-on lessons and much-needed support for new teachers. After 1 year of implementation, the district experienced a 30% increase in teacher retention (Lewis, 2006). The intensive program provided practical strategies in a variety of areas, including lesson planning, preparation, and instruction; the creation of student portfolios; classroom management and discipline; and communication with parents. The schools I observed used similar strategies, and they retained and empowered their new teachers as the catalysts for their school's cultural transformation.

A Multifaceted Approach to Mentoring

Some schools in this study felt that the traditional method of pairing a new teacher with one veteran mentor teacher was not adequate to strengthen the performance of their Tweeners. Two school principals and an associate superintendent identified new teacher development and retention as their top administrative priority. Their personal commitment and allocated resources were much higher than the other school leaders observed in this study. They felt as if it was the responsibility of the entire school community to embrace and develop newcomers. One elementary principal stated that teacher failure is worse than student failure: "When one student fails, that one student suffers, but when one teacher fails, 30 students fail."

One of the elementary schools in the study formed a New Teacher Committee. This committee consisted of the principal, three veteran teachers (all identified as Believers), the school counselor, and the main office secretary. Each member of this committee served a specific purpose in the development of all of the probationary teachers in the school.

The principal was responsible for the formal evaluation and pre- and post-evaluation conferences for each Tweener. The veteran teachers played a unique role. Each one was selected for a particular skill that distinguished him or her among the other teachers in the school. One was a master organizer, and her role was to work with all of the new teachers in the area of organizational skills. She guided them in everything from developing powerful and organized lesson plans to completing grading requirements for students. The second teacher was known as a master at creative pedagogy. She had done extensive research on learning styles and multiple intelligences and could take any lesson and make sure all student learning styles were being addressed. She modeled lessons for the new teachers and met with each one of them one on one on a weekly basis. The third teacher was master at student relations and discipline. He was well known by students and teachers as the teacher who connected best with students. He worked with the new teachers on classroom management. The counselor met with new teachers to coordinate support service needs, and the secretary made sure the new teachers stayed informed and did not drown in paperwork.

This system was extremely effective. This elementary school had a phenomenal retention rate of 100% over the next 7 years. Many of the Tweeners I interviewed at this school identified the committee as a powerful influence in their development. They also mentioned how their associates at other schools who did not receive this type of support were now looking to move to other professions.

Removing the Walls of Isolation

The second big idea in the PLC model developed by DuFour, DuFour, and Eaker is for schools to develop a culture of collaboration (2008). The entire PLC model is driven by the powerful paradigm that we are much more effective together than we are separately. Among the school leaders I observed, those who were most effective in this area were students of the PLC model, and they organized their schools into collaborative teams of teachers.

One high school principal was very methodical about how he assigned teachers to teams, especially new teachers. He had previously served as an assistant principal at another high school that was not quite as careful about how it assigned teachers to teams and how it monitored that process. He found that assigning teachers to unhealthy teams could produce more unhealthy teams. So when he became principal of his current school, he was careful how he exposed his new teachers. He made sure that new teachers were assigned to teams with a healthy and productive collaborative culture, instead of exposing them to less collaborative teams that might reinforce a culture he was working to change.

Teachers at this school were given 2 days per week to meet with colleagues during the school day in collaborative teams. On Tuesdays, teachers were assigned to content-specific teams. These team meetings were led by the subject department chairperson, and the agendas regularly included issues related to curriculum, assessments, instructional material, and pedagogy. On Thursdays, the veteran teachers met with other veteran content teachers to develop common formative assessments and review critical data. Simultaneously, the new teachers met with the department chairperson who advised them in all critical areas and allotted them time to ask questions without their veteran staff members present. This private collaboration made Tweeners comfortable with expressing frustrations and difficulty without the burden of judgment from the administration or veteran teachers. These collaborative sessions were very open and honest. Participants appreciated this opportunity, and many expressed that they looked forward to these weekly sessions.

This high school, like the elementary school identified earlier in this section, developed an excellent record of retaining new teachers. The principal began his tenure in 2002, inheriting 13 probationary teachers and hiring 11 more. Of the 24 new teachers under his leadership since his tenure began, 21 were still employed at the school at press time. Three are current department chairs, and one is currently serving as an assistant principal at the school. These new teachers evolved from novices to the shapers and messengers of the school norms.

Intensive Professional Development

One middle school principal in the study, a once-struggling new teacher himself, developed an intensive new teacher development program at his school. This principal, who once struggled with things like classroom management, lesson planning, and parent and community relations, admitted that these struggles almost drove him away from the profession. He admits that informal sessions with a teacher who taught in an adjacent classroom saved his career. The informal relationship was like a series of informative workshops on what he called "how to survive until you can thrive in the classroom." He vowed that if he became an administrator, he would never let new teachers struggle to learn basic things that all good teachers should know. He did not want his new teachers to be trained by happenstance; he wanted them to experience an *intentional* system of development.

This school leader starts this system early on—in fact, it is part of the new teacher interview process. He and his hiring team make sure they articulate to a prospective new teacher that he or she must be a learner as well as a teacher. Candidates who do not display a willingness to be perpetual learners are not considered for employment.

Once new teachers are hired, they are given a schedule of onsite professional development that they must attend every 2 weeks after school for 1 hour. These sessions are called "New Teacher Basic Training." The principal takes advantage of this military theme, weaving it throughout the language and promotion of the series. The topics for the sessions include:

- Classroom management
- Standardized testing
- Curriculum and standards
- Understanding the school system and how to get things done
- Understanding what constitutes good homework
- Communicating with parents
- Taking time for personal interests and development

These courses are taught by staff members at the school who have developed effective methods in each topic area. They are paid an extra financial stipend to teach the course. The program has grown from 3 sessions in 2001 to 21 sessions in 2006. This system brings out the best of both the new teachers and the veteran teachers, and the focus is on learning.

Effect on School Culture

This focus on the Tweeners empowers the Believers in a formal sense that gives them an official platform to push their paradigm. Socialization of new teachers is not left to chance. The most effective

Believers are given the time and opportunity to mold the new teachers in the belief systems that support the fundamental purpose of the school. The staff members who participate also display a proud "swagger"; they feel their productivity and commitment to the school goals is valued. The Believers in these schools, compared to others, are more willing to challenge Fundamentalists both in the formal and informal organizations.

Tweeners obviously benefit from these approaches. They have access to the experts in the school—not by chance, but by design. Not only do they receive guidance through modeling, but they also are systematically provided with time to ask impromptu questions and receive guidance by the teachers in their school who perform best in the most important areas of teaching.

This system causes Fundamentalists to lose valuable access to the driving force of their movement: impressionable Tweeners. This system restricts access to the Tweeners in the formal realm, which leaves only the informal. Tweeners interviewed at these schools made little mention of recruitment efforts by nonmentor staff members in informal situations. Fundamentalists were curious about what took place during the mentor-mentee sessions, but had little to no affect on the guidance and advice given by the Believers. The Believers in these schools provided the Tweeners with enough good guidance that even when they had their "moment of truth," the trust and confidence gained during regular mentoring and professional development sessions gave them the confidence to seek the advice of the building assigned experts, instead of seeking the guidance of a seemingly empathetic Fundamentalist.

Skillful Leadership and Focus

Transforming a toxic school culture marked by significant staff division into a healthy one does not happen by luck. Skillful leadership and a focus on key areas of school operation are critical to this process. A focus on learning, institutionalized celebration, and new teacher development are great places for school leaders to begin the quest for improved school culture. This chapter provides a research base and practical strategies that have been successful in reshaping school cultures. As school culture improves, students have a much better opportunity to learn in an environment that supports the practices that guarantee them a chance at success. The type of success they will enjoy will not be limited to just school; their success in the classroom will be the catalyst for their success in life.

EPILOGUE

A Significant Impact

As a former teacher and administrator, I can appreciate the challenges that educators face on a daily basis. It is not easy to work with students from diverse backgrounds and value systems and still create the harmonious school ethos and shared value system that the public expects. But if we are to be a society that mirrors this expectation we have of schools—diverse, just, and harmonious—we must transform our public school system to accomplish this end.

The purpose of this book is to stimulate conversation and inspire educators to analyze the impact of their belief systems on their practices, and how those practices impact their students. When students are nurtured in a culture where educators believe in their potential to do the extraordinary and work together to achieve this end, all children can be successful. This goal is hard to accomplish if the school staff is divided into four political groups with four different agendas. In a school culture where educators are aware of stereotypes, historical injustices, and the effects of being socialized in a class-based society, they are better prepared to create a healthy, nurturing environment for students—whether that school is located in an economically affluent suburb or in a housing project in an economically depressed inner city.

This issue is personal for me. I grew up in Flint, Michigan, in the 1970s. At the time of my childhood, Flint was a booming industrial center for General Motors. Employment opportunities were abundant, and the automotive industry fueled Flint's bustling economy. My home was right in the middle of a working-class neighborhood on the north end of Flint. When I was a child, the neighborhood was vibrant and alive with the laughter of children. I had four very close friends. We were inseparable, and we had hopes and dreams of becoming great one day and making our mark on the world. My friends came from very close-knit families that provided all the love and support that a young man would need. Their home was like mine, except for one very critical difference.

The parents of my close friends all worked at the various General Motors plants around Flint, except one mother, who was a homemaker. Of the seven parents that worked in the factory, only three graduated from high school, and the remaining four did not complete their high school education, yet the abundant opportunities offered by the automotive industry provided each household with a very comfortable, middle-class income. My mother was different in our neighborhood because she was the only person that did not work in the auto industry; she was a teacher in the Flint Public Schools. She eventually earned her master's degree in education, but despite her education, her income did not come close to matching an income from factory wages. So even though my mother was highly educated, we were poor compared to my neighbors.

This difference also set up a different set of expectations in school where achievement was concerned. The homes where my best friends were reared did not enjoy a middle-class lifestyle through the traditional means of using education as the vehicle for social mobility. Their income rose as a result of the prosperity of the American automotive industry, therefore there was not a connection between education and quality of life. All of my friends' parents valued education, as do the vast majority of parents regardless of social class, but they were caught in the mirage that the American automotive industry would always be prosperous and that their children would one day inherit their jobs. Their parents wanted them to do well in school, but there was no real sense of urgency where achievement was concerned. My home was very different. My mother set very high and rigid standards for school performance for me and my siblings. We were given no option where school performance was concerned.

My buddies and I all attended the same schools and were exposed to the same things at school and in the neighborhood. We were all ambitious and vibrant. There was no real difference in ability or intellect.

We achieved in school at nearly the same level until about fourth grade. At that point, I was pushed on to an honors track, and they were on the average track. One of my friends was placed in special education. By high school, the differences were more pronounced, and I was a part of a very small group of honor students. By the end of high school, only three of us graduated. I was the only one of the group who went to college. Our schools presented us with opportunities for high achievement for those who were interested, but with the automotive industry at its peak, many of my classmates chose to drop out of school and go work in the factories. This was such a normal part of the culture of my city that very few people inside or outside the school system seemed to be alarmed.

The culture that we experienced within the walls of our schools sent different messages to us. There was a core group of Believers, which we appreciated, and they inspired us to achieve even though many students would not pursue advanced learning opportunities and would work in the factories. There were definitely Tweeners and pockets of Survivors, but the Fundamentalists were also present. Their Social Darwinist characteristics discouraged many of my friends, and I personally witnessed discouraging and damaging commentary from them. They articulated in subtle and overt ways that the factory was our best option, and that that was just how the world worked. Many of us developed an animosity for these members of the faculty as well as a dislike for school in general. One of my friends quit high school because of this feeling of being unwanted because he did not fit the right profile.

In the mid-1980s, the American automotive industry took a major blow. Declining sales, rising costs, and foreign competition caused General Motors and other manufacturers to close plants and eliminate jobs. The jobs that my friends and their families thought would be there forever were gone. Plant closings in Flint came fast and furious, and my friends found themselves with very little education in a world with few job options. Today, two of my friends are no longer alive, one is incarcerated, and the fourth friend is trying to make ends meet through temporary employment. I have enjoyed an exciting career in education and have achieved even more than I could ever have dreamed as a child. Why is there such a difference in the trajectory of our lives?

It is not because of abilities or greater intellect. I grew up in a healthy home culture where education was valued, and my education has been the foundation of my adult life.

This was not a prevailing paradigm in the homes of many of my friends, and, unfortunately, not even in many of the classrooms that we attended as students in our local schools. My friends were left vulnerable to the ills associated with low academic achievement that are outlined in chapter 1. This left a lasting impression on me. All students deserve a quality education despite their level of interest and parental involvement—this is an imperative in the 21st century and beyond. When human beings are at their best, they are thoughtful, ethical, productive, and humane, and a quality education can produce all of these attributes. My greatest hope is that educators grasp this concept and universally dedicate themselves to creating schools that provide adequate guidance and support for all kids, and that they aspire to become the transformational institutions that make the community a better place to live in and our world a better place.

APPENDIX

Study Design

Sample

This study was conducted by collecting data from 34 public schools in the United States scattered across four regions (see the table on page 123). Those regions were East, Midwest, South, and West. The sample included 11 elementary schools, 14 middle schools, and 9 high schools. These schools ranged in student enrollment from small (200–400), medium (401–1,000), and large (1,001+). Student socioeconomic status spanned poor (50%+ students receiving free and reduced lunch), moderate (10%–49%), and affluent (9% or less). Student racial population ranged from diverse (more than two racial groups of 25% or more), moderate (three or more racial groups of 10% or more), and homogeneous (one racial group more than 90% of student population).

Data Collection

This study was an ethnography, and data was collected using three methods. The data was collected over a 3-year period from 2004–2007. Informal observations of classrooms in session during regular school hours, staff meetings, teacher team meetings, and other formal and informal gatherings of staff members were used to collect observational data. Formal interviews were conducted with each building principal and a randomly chosen group of teachers at each school. Each interviewee was asked the same questions, and his or her answers were tape-recorded. A document review was done at each site. These documents included student grade reports, student and staff attendance reports, and standardized test results. The names of staff members and students were kept confidential on all reports provided by building and district administration.

Variables

This study examined two aspects of school culture: political objective and political motivation. The researcher used the data collected to determine the objective or organizational goal of the educator through examining their interaction with all members of the organizations and correlating the observed behaviors with stated objectives during formal interviews and document and data reviews. A series of independent or predictor variables was created from the data collected. Once the political objective/category was determined, the researcher sought to identify the motivation of the educator through examination of literature and theory related to organizational behavior in currently published sociological literature.

Schools in the Study and Their Demographic Data

School	Region	Size	Socioeconomic Status	Racial Diversity
Elementary A	Midwest	Small	Moderate	Homogeneous
Elementary B	South	Medium	Moderate	Diverse
Elementary C	South	Small	Poor	Diverse
Elementary D	West	Small	Affluent	Diverse
Elementary E	Midwest	Small	Moderate	Moderate
Elementary F	Midwest	Medium	Moderate	Diverse
Elementary G	East	Medium	Poor	Homogeneous
Elementary H	Midwest	Small	Poor	Homogeneous
Elementary I	East	Medium	Affluent	Homogeneous
Elementary J	West	Small	Poor	Diverse
Elementary K	Midwest	Small	Moderate	Diverse
Middle School A	Midwest	Medium	Poor	Homogeneous
Middle School B	East	Medium	Moderate	Moderate
Middle School C	East	Large	Moderate	Moderate
Middle School D	South	Medium	Poor	Diverse
Middle School E	West	Medium	Poor	Homogeneous
Middle School F	Midwest	Large	Affluent	Homogeneous
Middle School G	Midwest	Medium	Moderate	Moderate
Middle School H	Midwest	Small	Poor	Homogeneous
Middle School I	South	Medium	Moderate	Diverse
Middle School J	West	Medium	Poor	Moderate
Middle School K	West	Medium	Moderate	Moderate
Middle School L	East	Large	Affluent	Homogeneous
Middle School M	Midwest	Large	Moderate	Homogeneous
Middle School N	Midwest	Medium	Moderate	Moderate
High School A	South	Medium	Moderate	Diverse
High School B	West	Large	Moderate	Moderate
High School C	Midwest	Large	Moderate	Homogeneous
High School D	East	Large	Affluent	Homogeneous
High School E	Midwest	Large	Poor	Homogeneous
High School F	Midwest	Medium	Moderate	Moderate
High School G	Midwest	Large	Affluent	Homogeneous
High School H	South	Large	Moderate	Homogeneous
High School I	Midwest	Small	Moderate	Diverse

References

Allen, J. (2007). Inequality in funding of public education raises justice issues: Quality often depends on where students live. *National Catholic Reporter, 2, 3.*

Allen, M. B. (2005). *Eight questions on teacher recruitment and retention: What does the research say?* Washington, DC: Education Commission of the States.

Applied Research Center. (2000). *Facing the consequences: An examination of racial discrimination in the public schools.* Oakland, CA: Applied Research Center.

Associated Press. (2003, January 29). Report: Teacher retention biggest school woe. *CNN.com/Education.* Accessed at www.cnn.com/2003/EDUCATION/01/29/teacher.shortage.ap/ on October 27, 2008.

Baldoni, J. (2007, October 3). *Leadership: Trust matters. Fast company: Grab 'n go leadership.* Accessed at www.fastcompany.com/blog/john-baldoni/grab-n-go-leadership/leadership-trust-matters on October 27, 2008.

Bannister, R. C. (2008). Social Darwinism. In *Microsoft Encarta Online Encyclopedia.* Accessed at http://encarta.msn.com on October 27, 2008.

Barnes, G., Schaefer, B., & Crowe, E. (2007). *The cost of teacher turnover in five school districts.* Washington, DC: National Commission on Teaching and America's Future.

Barr, G. (2008). Study: Texas school system fosters low graduation rates. *Dallas Business Journal.* Accessed at http://www.bizjournals.com/dallas/stories/2008/02/11/daily36.html on October 10, 2008.

Bolman, L., & Deal, T. (1995). *Leading with soul: An uncommon journey of spirit.* San Francisco: Jossey-Bass.

Buffum, A., Erkens, C., Hinman, C., Huff, S., Jessie, L. G., Martin, T. L., Mattos, M., Muhammad, A., Noonan, P., Parscale, G., Twadell, E., Westover, J., & Williams, K. C. (2008). *The collaborative administrator: Working together as a professional learning community.* Bloomington, IN: Solution Tree Press.

Burnham, T., & Johnson, D. (2005). The biological and evolutionary logic of human cooperation. *Analyse and Kritik, 27,* 113–125.

Butler, J., & Dickson, K. (1987). *Improving school culture: School improvement research series.* Portland, OR: Northwest Regional Educational Laboratory.

Chang, W. H., Park, J. J., & Shim, S. (1998). Effectiveness of negative political advertising. *Web Journal of Mass Communication Research, 2*(1), 17.

Christensen, F. (2008, August 5). *New teachers: Alone in the classroom, together in the chatroom.* California Virtual Campus. Accessed at www.cvc.edu/faculty/articles-opinions/posts/new-teachers-alone-in-the-classroom-together-in-the-chatroom on October 27, 2008.

Collins, J. (2001). *Good to great: Why some companies make the leap . . . and others don't.* New York: Harper Business.

Cotton, K. (1989). *Expectations and student outcomes: School improvement research series.* Portland, OR: Northwest Regional Educational Laboratory.

Covey, S. (1989). *The seven habits of highly effective people.* New York: Free Press.

Cromwell, S. (2002). Is your school culture toxic or positive? *Education World, 6*(2), 1.

Cuban, L., & Tyack, D. (1995). *Tinkering towards utopia: A century of public school reform.* Cambridge: Harvard University Press.

Dizon, N. Z., Feller, B., & Bass, F. (2006, April 18). *States omitting minorities' test scores.* Associated Press. Accessed at www.boston.com/news/education/k_12/articles/2006/04/18/ap_states_omit_minorities_school_scores/ on October 27, 2008.

Dodge, W. (1949). *Testimony. Mann Gulch transcript* (pp. 117–125). Washington, DC: U.S. Forest Service.

DuFour, R. (2001). Community: Getting everyone to buy in. *Journal of Staff Development, 22*(4), 3.

DuFour, R. (2002). One clear voice is needed in the din. *Journal of Staff Development, 23*(2), 4.

DuFour, R., & DuFour, R. (2006). The power of professional learning communities. *National Forum of Educational Administration and Supervision Journal, 24*(1), 2–5.

DuFour, R., DuFour, R., & Eaker, R. (2008). *Revisiting professional learning communities at work: New insights for improving schools.* Bloomington, IN: Solution Tree Press.

DuFour, R., & Eaker, R. (1998). *Professional learning communities at work: Best practices for enhancing student achievement.* Bloomington, IN: Solution Tree Press (formerly National Educational Service).

Feller, B. (2006, April 20). *AP poll: Teachers dubious of 'No Child.'* Associated Press. Accessed at www.highbeam.com/doc/1P1–122146681.html on October 27, 2008.

Ferguson, R. (1998, April 7). Teacher perceptions, expectations, and behaviors may put black students at a disadvantage. *The Achievement Gap*, 27–31.

Friedman, T. (2005). *The world is flat.* Farrar, Straus and Giroux

Fullan, M. (2003). *The moral imperative of school leadership.* Thousand Oakes, CA: Corwin Press.

Glanz, B. (2000). Improve morale to increase productivity. *Innovative Leader, 9*(7), 8.

Green, R. (2005). *Expectations: How teacher expectations can increase student achievement and assist in closing the achievement gap.* Columbus, OH: SRA McGraw-Hill.

Haberman, M. (2005). Teacher burnout in black and white. *The New Educator, 1*(3), 153–175.

Helfand, D. (2005, November 17). Researchers say teachers unions hurt the children in big cities. *Los Angeles Times.*

Herrnstein, R., & Murray, C. (1994). *The bell curve: Intelligence and class structure in American life.* New York: Free Press.

Higgins, L., & Pratt-Dawsey, C. (2008, April 23). Changes to No Child unveiled. *Detroit Free Press*, 177, 1.

Hudson, C. (2005). Socioeconomic status and mental illness. *American Journal of Orthopsychiatry, 75*(1), 14–17.

Hunt, J. (2003). Teacher retention biggest school woe. Accessed at http://www.cnn.com/2003/EDUCATION/01/29/teacher.shortage.ap/ on July 19, 2008.

Infoplease. (2006). African-Americans by the numbers: U.S. Census. Accessed at http://www.infoplease.com/spot/bhmcensus1.html on September 9, 2008.

Jencks, C., & Phillips, M. (1998). *The black-white test score gap: An introduction.* Washington, DC: Brookings Institution.

Jones, M. T. (2008). Race/ethnicity and teacher expectations of college attendance. American Sociological Association Annual Conference. Montreal, Quebec: 27.

Keller, B. (2008). Studies link teacher absences to lower student scores. *Education Week, 27,* 1.

Kennedy, M. (2005). *Inside teaching: How classroom life undermines reform.* Cambridge, MA: Harvard University Press.

Kopkowski, C. (2008, February). Why they leave: Lack of respect, NCLB, and underfunding—in a topsy-turvy profession, what can make today's teachers stay? NEA Today. Accessed at www.nea.org/neatoday/0804/whytheyleave.html on October 27, 2008.

Kunjufu, J. (2002). *Black students, middle class teachers.* Chicago: African American Images.

Learning Point Associates. (n.d.). *Teacher perceptions, expectations, and behaviors may put black students at a disadvantage.* Achievement Gaps. Accessed at http://lpadev.learningpt.org/gaplibrary/text/teacherperceptions2.php on October 27, 2008.

Levin, H. (2006). Equity by the numbers. *Phi Delta Kappan, 13,* 53–65.

Lewis, L. (2006). Baltimore program helps new teachers get off to a good start. *Education World, 3,* 11–12.

Lortie, D. (1975). *Schoolteacher: A sociological study.* Chicago: University of Chicago Press.

Maccoby, M. (2008). Schools need collaborative leaders. *Education Week, 27*(24), 11.

Maclean, N. (1992). *Young men and fire.* Chicago: University of Chicago Press.

Merriam-Webster OnLine. (2008). Accessed at www.merriam-webster.com on October 27, 2008.

Moire, E. (2008, Winter). Building an effective new teacher support system. *NEA Today: Issues in Education Report, 7.*

National Commission on Teaching and America's Future. (2003). *No dream denied: A pledge to American children.* Washington, DC: Author.

Nelson, N. C. (2007). *The power of appreciation in business.* New York: MindLab Publishing.

Ogbu, J. (2003). *Black American students in an affluent suburb: A study of academic disengagement.* New York: Lawrence Erlbaum Associates.

Pyoria, P. (2007). Informal organizational culture: The foundation of knowledge workers' performance. *Journal of Knowledge Management, 11*(3), 16–30.

Sadovi, C. (2008, September 8). Chicago students skip for a cause. *Chicago Tribune.*

Sallee, R. (1949). *Testimony. Mann Gulch transcript* (pp. 69–89). Washington, DC: U.S. Forest Service.

Samples, J. (2006). *The fallacy of campaign financing reform.* Chicago: University of Chicago Press.

Sanders, W., & Rivers, J. (1996). *Cumulative and residual effects of teachers on future student academic achievement.* Knoxville: University of Tennessee.

Shaw, B. (2008, March 12). Our nation still at risk. *Education Week*, 17–18.

Smith, M., Jaffe-Gill, E., Segal, J., & Segal, R. (2007, October 26). *Preventing burnout: Signs, symptoms, and strategies to avoid it.* Helpguide.org. Accessed at www.helpguide.org/mental/burnout_signs_symptoms.htm on October 27, 2008.

Sparks, D. (2002). *High-performing cultures increase teacher retention.* Oxford, OH: National Staff Development Council.

Study: Texas system fosters low graduation rates. (2008, February 15). *Austin Business Journal.*

Tangredi, D. (2005, January 29). Einstein: Definition of insanity. *Ezine Articles.* Accessed at http://ezinearticles.com/?expert=Danny_Tangredi on October 27, 2008.

Toppo, G. (2008, May 1). Study: Reading First has little impact on kids' scores. *USA Today.*

U.S. Department of Defense. (1973). *Military leadership.* Annapolis, MD: Author.

U.S. Forest Service. (1949). *Mann Gulch transcript.* Washington, DC: Author.

U.S. Forest Service. (1994). *Report of the South Canyon Fire Accident Investigation Team.* Washington, DC: Author.

Weick, K. E. (1996). Drop your tools: An allegory for organizational studies. *Administrative Science Quarterly, 41,* 301–313. Accessed at http://findarticles.com/p/articles/mi_m4035/is_n2_v41/ai_18555964/pg_6?tag=artBody;col1 (at BNET Business Network) on January 23, 2009.

Wilson, B. L., & Corbett, H. D. (2001). *Listening to urban kids: School reform and the teachers they want.* Albany: State University of New York Press.

Winerip, M. (2007, December 9). In gaps at school, weighing family life. *The New York Times.*

Wood, T., & McCarthy-Wood, C. (2002). *Understanding and preventing teacher burnout. Washington, DC: ERIC Clearinghouse on Teaching and Teacher Education.* (ERIC Document Reproduction Service No. ED477726) Accessed at www.ericdigests.org/2004–1/burnout.htm on October 27, 2008.

Wynn, S. (2006, April 12). Principal leadership, school climate critical to retaining beginning teachers, Duke study finds. *Duke News.*

Zuckerbrod, N. (2007, November 15). *City schools gain, yet still lag nation.* AP News. Accessed at www.thefreelibrary.com/NANCY+ZUCKERBROD-a1449 on October 27, 2008.

Ahead of the Curve: The Power of Assessment to Transform Teaching and Learning
Edited by Douglas Reeves
Leaders in education contribute their perspectives of effective assessment design and implementation, sending out a call for redirecting assessment to improve student achievement and inform instruction.
BKF232

Revisiting Professional Learning Communities at Work™: New Insights for Improving Schools
Richard DuFour, Rebecca DuFour, and Robert Eaker
This 10th anniversary sequel to *Professional Learning Communities at Work™* offers advanced insights on deep implementation, the commitment/consensus issue, and the human side of PLC. **BKF252**

Change Wars
Edited by Michael Fullan and Andy Hargreaves
In the third Leading Edge™ anthology, education luminaries from around the globe share their theories-in-action on how to achieve deep change. **BKF254**

The Collaborative Administrator
Austin Buffum, Cassandra Erkens, Charles Hinman, Susan Huff, Lillie G. Jessie, Terri L. Martin, Mike Mattos, Anthony Muhammad, Peter Noonan, Geri Parscale, Eric Twadell, Jay Westover, and Kenneth C. Williams
Foreword by Robert Eaker
In a culture of shared leadership, the administrator's role is more important than ever. This book addresses your toughest challenges with practical strategies and inspiring insight. **BKF256**

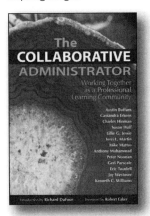